UPSIDE-DOWN
UPSIDE-DOWN

Strategic Planning

From Values to Vision to
Transformation

Bob and Linda Ryan

Market 70 International

Copyright

Upside-Down Strategic Planning

Acknowledgements

This book would not have been possible without the many clients who have worked with us in Upside-Down Strategic Planning. Thank you.

Also, thanks to the many volunteer readers who gave us invaluable feedback both in style and in copy editing. Finally, a special thanks to Ted Sheppard of T Sheppard Photography for his excellent work on the cover.

Table of Contents

Introduction

Our 7 year-old granddaughter is a very active child. She seems to spend more time topsy-turvy, rolling around on the floor than she spends on her feet. One day, from her upside-down perspective, she announced she could clearly see the outside under the French doors of our new house – not a good thing in Minnesota where the north winds can make winter quite uncomfortable. Sure enough, we inspected the door only to find a ½" gap running six feet along the bottom of the door, which we quickly patched up with insulation.

That experience confirmed for us the value of the model of strategic planning we teach. Flipped upside-down from the traditional model of strategic planning, we have found that the perspective it brings to organizations is invaluable. It introduces a fresh understanding of mission that energizes employees and gives new direction to management.

If you work in a company of any size, you have probably participated in a strategic planning session. Government, businesses, churches and education all do strategic planning. Many engage consultants to guide them through the process. Large organizations have departments that are dedicated to ongoing strategic planning and to watching over the implementation of the plans.

The process is very helpful and if done right, empowers and encourages the participants. When employees and other stakeholders take part in the process, we often see improved "ownership" of the purposes and goals of the organization. A good strategic plan informs the direction of the organization and provides guidance for action.

If done poorly, on the other hand, the process seems to discourage participants and has the overall effect of injecting hopelessness and inactivity. Hours and weeks of work go into writing a tome that then sits on a shelf until the next year. A bad strategic plan, rather than providing direction, creates expectations that cannot possibly be accomplished and contributes to a sense that the organization cannot meet its mission.

Many have asked us to put Upside-Down Strategic Planning into a book so that they can continue using the process regularly and build it into their annual planning as well as employ it all year long as an effective decision-making tool. You now have this book in your hands. But is it for you?

Our perspective is clearly from a Christian, Biblical point of view. Those of you who are comfortable with that will find great insights from the Scriptural foundations for the process. However, those of you who are not will still find common-sense value in the process if you look at it from a purely practical point of view. We have used the Upside-Down process with "secular" organizations, including units of government, and the participants have all found it extremely helpful. The principles are sound even if you don't get excited about how we discovered them.

As we all know, ideas, principles and insights can come from unexpected places, as they did with us in this upside-down approach. We hope that all our readers might attempt discovery in these pages, even if the source of the ideas might not be familiar or even appealing to you.

At various places, we offer different ways to understand these principles in highlighted text. We also invite you to read Appendix 2.

So, with an open mind, we invite you to roll around on the floor with us and look at your organization from a new perspective – upside-down.

Chapter One

Our Journey to Turning Ourselves Upside-Down

The Birth of Market 70

Early in 2011, we joined our church in a 40-day Daniel fast – a time of limiting eating to the essentials so that we could focus our minds and hearts on renewed purpose and direction. Much to our surprise, we were led to narrow our management 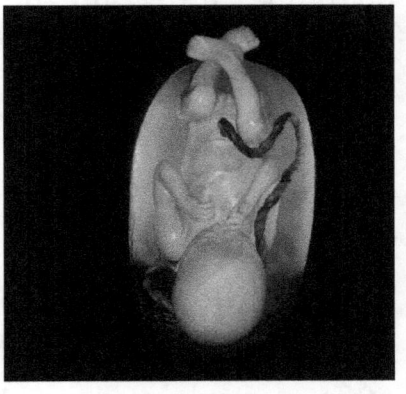 consulting business to a much smaller niche. We were to begin working with Christian-led or Christian-owned organizations that were committed to being intentionally transformative – that is, to changing the world around them through their marketplace activity.

About this time we entered into something you might find familiar – we argued with God. We reasoned that He hadn't been hanging around in the marketplace, so perhaps He had lost touch with how business really works. We explained that narrowing our consulting niche – especially to one so minimally defined – would seriously limit our revenue potential. But like everyone before us who doubted God's wisdom, we lost the argument. We surrendered the franchise we owned, giving up about 85% of our income, and launched Market 70 International.

On the positive side, that began a whirlwind of activity in which insights and ideas around building intentionally transformative organizations literally poured out over us. There were times when we would sit across the table from each other, furiously pounding away on our laptops to capture the download of insight and wisdom God was giving us.

"Listen to this! I just got this incredible idea about marketing!"

"No, wait! First you have to hear these ideas on creating an intercessory team!"

We were practically tripping over each other's words in our excitement to record all we were hearing.

After a couple of days, we got to the part where we needed to create a section on strategic planning for the new website. After all, I'd been teaching and leading strategic planning through my whole consulting career. I remember telling Linda, "Why don't you take a break and relax? I've got this stuff down cold. I'll write it up and have it uploaded in a couple of hours."

Two days later... I still had nothing. Every time I started to write down what I've known and experienced during my whole consulting career, it fizzled. It would just not come together. I finally had to admit defeat. I thought, "How could this be? I've done this for almost 30 years. How could I be getting a complete block?

Have you ever had one of those times in your life when you suddenly realized you were going about something all wrong? Well, this was one of those moments. I saw in a flash what was wrong. I was trying to do what I had always done. Even though it had been very successful and was based in good, solid research and practice, it wasn't consistent with what God was trying to do with Market 70. He was revealing something new. He was leading us down innovative paths. He didn't want what we had done in the past. He wanted what He would do in the future.

We closed our laptops and prayed. Then we just sat and listened. And we got the words, "Upside-down." Upside-down? What is upside-down? We kept going over the essentials – Mission, Vision, Values. Mission, Vision, Values. And then we saw it. Upside-down would be Values/Vision/Mission. We went back to the laptops with a listening ear and it began to flow.

The strategic planning model He wanted us to use flips the world model upside-down. Instead of starting with our mission, we were to start with values. Not our values – His values. Once we saw His values, a new vision emerged. Not our vision – His vision. As we got excited about that novel vision, our mission became clear. We will share the Upside-Down model with you in Chapters 4-6.

Having experienced such an epiphany, we became better conduits for revelation. After the excitement of the upside-down realization, we came to the next logical step in strategic planning – the SWOT analysis. For those of you who don't know, that stands for Strengths, Weaknesses, Opportunities, and Threats. Once again, we were stopped dead in our tracks. This time, we were wise enough to ask, "Why?" and listen for an answer. God gave us a revelation about SWOT that flies in the face of conventional wisdom. We went back to the laptop and were pleased to receive a fresh download.

In short, we learned that SWOT thwarts the creative process by shifting our attention to the negatives. It focuses us on the stumbling blocks before our eyes rather than on the prize. SWOT is concerned with what is in the current system. We are called to transformation; to restoring that which has been destroyed; to healing that which is broken. (Luke 4:18-19, Luke 19:10 and John 17:18). Christians believe Christ came to redeem the world, reclaiming all that had been spoiled. He passed on that mission to us. This really challenged our thoughts and opened up new ways for us to see our own planning, as well as teach it to others. We will share more about that in Chapter 7.

The remainder of the planning process follows the model the world is used to – but it rolls out very differently because of the upside-down start. The big picture is clearly stamped on everyone's hearts and minds. Where goals, strategies and action plans focus only on the positive outcomes, staff energy and corporate resources are fully released. The upside-down perspective brings fresh excitement and ownership.

Growing up, Upside-Down

Having experienced this innovative new approach to something as tried and true as strategic planning had been for our whole career, we were anxious to move on to the rest of the steps in becoming intentionally transformative. We continued our listening process, acting as scribes and recording all that was unfolding before us. And we were not disappointed. We were led to view many other things from this upside-down perspective.

Leadership has often been approached from an upside-down view. Servant leadership, inverted triangles, employee ownership and many more enlightened models of leadership have emerged over the years. But, even in this area, we were surprised to see yet a fresh perspective flowing out of the upside-down mindset. Of course leadership is to serve the mission and the stakeholders, but primarily leadership is to shepherd and promote the values that define the vision. Leading from the values drives planning and execution. It drives human resource acquisition, training and development. It drives governance and succession planning.

We moved on to marketing and again saw the wisdom of the upside-down perspective. Rather than marketing a service or product, we found we were being led to position the values as the end-goal.

Similar to the discipline of branding, but with a distinct difference. We were not positioning ourselves in the mind of the customer, but rather we were branding a vision far wider than anything we could represent. We were positioning the organization for transformation.

This realization went on to all the other parts of organizational structure and activities from sales to finance, from procurement to credit policy, from HR practices to mergers and acquisitions. The upside-down perspective redefines everything about the organization and how it interfaces with its sphere of influence.

From the childlike practice of "rolling around on the floor," we were learning an entire discipline of looking at things upside-down.

As Christians, we understand that we are being "led by the Spirit," a phrase which means that we have moved beyond our own understanding and have stepped into a realm in which we see things from an eternal, spiritual perspective. We began to realize that the "upside" part of our vision was a Kingdom viewpoint. We were sharing in the perspective of the King of the universe.

If the "upside" is the Kingdom perspective, then the "down" part is the application of the Kingdom in the here and now, on earth. Much has been written about the "now and coming Kingdom," but most agree that God's intention is that we experience the benefits of the Kingdom in the present, as well as in eternity. We find that the upside-down perspective is teaching us how to apply and enjoy those benefits through the marketplace.

This should also give you some insight into the power of the Upside-Down model for strategic planning. It calls out the perfect future in the midst of the imperfect present. It leads us to see our organization as a finished product – the way it is going to be when we complete the goals, strategies and action plans that will fulfill the vision of the future. With this outlook, we begin to experience the outcome before it is fully realized. We share in the pride of what it is to become. We begin aligning our behavior with the truth of the future rather than with limitation of the past and present.

We are growing up, upside-down and are finding it to be highly effective and totally delightful. We invite you to share the journey with us. Come on! Turn some somersaults with us! Get upside-down with us.

Chapter Two

Failing to Plan is Planning to Fail

Some say that if you know what you're doing, planning isn't really necessary. Others say planning is a waste of time. Still others point to massive strategic plan documents sitting on office shelves and assert that plans are not being used anyway. Some say that planning is a sure sign that you don't trust God. They maintain the Bible already has everything in it you need to know. And all of those people are right! Well, partially right.

"If you don't know where you are going, you'll end up someplace else."
— Yogi Berra

Let's establish this right away. Planning is necessary and planning is Biblical.

There is a difference between the words "planning" and "plan." Planning is a verb; a process; a dynamic interchange between people, situations and resources.

Plan is a noun, an outcome of the process; and is only as valuable as the adjectives describing its development and the will of people to use it. Those critics of strategic planning are most often confusing the plan with the planning.

Those who say planning isn't necessary if you know what you're doing are just not aware of the process because of their familiarity with what's needed for success. Their plan works because they have engaged in successful, subconscious planning. But they are discounting the valuable time wasted fixing avoidable mistakes and adjusting to changing circumstances that could have been foreseen.

Those who rightfully discount the plans on office shelves are victims of a poor planning process that created a document rather than a living organism that continually examines and updates itself to fit changing circumstances.

Those who have religious objections correctly lift up the value of trusting that God is in control and will make all things perfect in the end. However, this often results in abdicating our responsibility to steward the earth and to call the Kingdom into being in the here and now.

Planning? Action? Or Both?

There are two important factors to consider in answering this question. The first is what we call the Effort/Effect factor and the second is what we call the Reliance factor.

The Effort/Effect factor weighs the amount of effort needed for planning with the effect of the outcome. For example, if the outcome of an action has very little effect on you or your organization or your family, then the amount of effort worth putting in is very little. If I

Effort/Effect Factor

	High Effect	Low Effect
High Effort	Will result in some measurable change important to the organization, promoting values and shepherding resources.	May use undue amount of resources accomplishing little or nothing of worth in organization values.
Low Effort	Will risk violating values, jeopardizing mission, and squandering resources.	Could result in outcomes that have little or no effect on either values or resources.

want to buy a screw driver just to have an extra in the kitchen for those few times anyone will use it, then it doesn't make sense to do hours of research on the types of screwdrivers, the brands offered, the quality vs. price issue, etc. I certainly will not want to put any effort into designing a screw driver safety program, training and orientation, and a protocol for borrowing and returning the screw driver to a designated storage spot.

On the other hand, if I want to build a workshop onto my house, it will be vital that I do extensive research and perhaps hire an architect. I will need to study building codes, financing options and effects on resale values. I will want to study all the available tools, their features and benefits and the specs on their size, use, etc.

The **Hi Effort/Hi Effect** quadrant falls under the old saying, "Anything worth doing is worth doing well." In his book, *Seven Habits of Highly Effective People*, Stephen Covey graphed Importance and Urgency. He suggests that we try to shift all of our efforts to those things that are important, but not urgent. To accomplish that we must focus our planning on longer-term decisions that give substance to the future of our organizations, our families and our communities. We must pay constant attention to the values that give meaning to our vision and mission. This is one of the reasons for "Upside-Down" Strategic Planning. It keeps the values in front of our face throughout all our decision making. It directs our highest efforts to those things with the highest effect.

The **Low Effort/High Effect** quadrant becomes a dangerous trap. Not putting enough effort into those things which are essential to our beliefs will certainly begin a downward spiral that could destroy us. Peter Greer wrote a book called *Mission Drift* in which he describes how easy it is for organizations to lose their way because of not putting enough effort into making sure that the values that underlie the mission are being constantly upheld. It is natural to take the path of least resistance. Corporations see a quick and ready revenue source and embrace it because it takes little or no effort on their part. In doing so, they may sacrifice a key value that had defined their brand for generations.

Both of the right side, **Low Effect quadrants** might suggest there are some things that don't need any planning. However, be careful of the Law of Unintended Consequences. Ignoring any planning could still have negative effects. Covey's model would suggest that a judicious use of effort in the Low Effect categories could keep things from becoming Urgent and force us to steal valuable time away from those things which are Important. Buying a magnetic screwdriver could ruin some of the other things I keep in the junk drawer. Intentionally undertaking the discipline of a planning process – even a basic one – could reveal things you may not have thought of, saving you time, money and heartache in the long run.

The other factor that influences the planning vs. action question is the Reliance Factor, which you will see influences the Effort/Effect factor.

The Reliance factor weighs the amount of skills, knowledge and resources you have with those that are available through other sources. Simply put, to guarantee a good outcome, it suggests that the experience must come from somewhere, either internally or externally. The intimacy one has with that source determines how much effort is put into the planning process and the amount of reliance that is put into other sources.

When we decided to put an addition onto our house, I would either need the skills and knowledge or I'd need to rely on someone who does have them. My brother-in-law was an invaluable asset to me in installing the electrical circuitry needed for our new kitchen. He had the experience, the tools, and the knowledge. With that, he helped me plan and execute what has been a wonderful result. Yet even with his help, we found that there was no substitute for the knowledge and experience of the city electrical inspector. Several things had been developed and written into code that we did not know. We had to spend extra money to fix those things we thought we had done right. That showed a hole in our planning due to low external reliance. We were not intimately associated with the laws and best practices, and relied only on our own knowledge.

That's an example of how the Reliance Factor influences the Effort/Effect factor. Had we relied less on our own knowledge and experience, we may have put more effort into researching recent codes. By doing so, we would have saved money and hours of extra work.

We could have ignored the inspector's warnings and risked punishment in fines if we were found out. Even if we weren't, there could have been injuries or property damage. Or lower resale value when a new buyer discovered the shortcut. So we had to put more effort in our planning so that a safe and legal effect was accomplished.

The more intimate we are with the sources of knowledge, experience and resources, the better our planning will be. **High External/High Internal Reliance** will always bring the highest quality results. It may seem duplicative at times but it is the best way to ensure our values will be upheld. Internal participants in the planning process are immersed in every phase of the organization, and bringing in external participants provides subject knowledge specific to the activity area being planned.

Reliance Factor		
	High External Reliance	Low External Reliance
High Internal Reliance	Will result in excellence with little chance of unintended consequences. May use high resources initially, but preserve resources over time.	Outcome more dependent on quality of skills and resources available internally. Can distract from organization mission.
Low Internal Reliance	Relies on external knowledge and skill but could expose organization to incompatible values and exorbitant costs.	Will likely result in mission paralysis and sacrifice of values. Outcomes will either not get accomplished or quality will be low.

High External/Low Internal Reliance has the advantage of letting the experts do what the experts do best. But it runs the risk of putting important decisions in the hands of people who don't necessarily share the values on which we have founded our vision and mission. There must be someone with internal expertise who can hold every phase of the planning up to the values and rigorously examine the effect of any action recommendations.

The Lo External/Hi Internal Reliance quadrant has its own hidden danger. Our self-reliance can deceive us into thinking we know more than we do. It can blind us to circumstances around us that have changed. It can keep us from recognizing and responding to important trends. That very same self-confidence which is so important to keep us going can become our biggest enemy.

A popular model that helps to explain this is the "Conscious Competence" model. There is much confusion on the origins, so we can't credit the author, but the model describes the way competence is built.

Unconsciously Incompetent

Consciously Incompetent

Consciously Competent

Unconsciously Competent

First, we are unconsciously incompetent – that is, we don't know what we don't know. We are not even aware there is something we are not doing correctly. Then, something or someone makes us consciously incompetent – showing us what it is that we are doing poorly. If we are open, we learn from that and become consciously competent, practicing the new skill or exercising the new knowledge in a purposeful way. Finally, as we internalize it, we become unconsciously competent.

This progression keeps repeating itself until we die. This suggests that we will always have areas in which we are not aware that we lack knowledge or skills. That being true, we have to question, "From which Reliance quadrant ought we to be planning? Do we assume comprehensive abilities and 'shoot from the hip?' Or do we seek input from someone likely to have more maturity in matters than we do?" By increasing consciousness of our level of competence, we are likely to produce better planning and therefore, a better outcome.

Planning? Or The Plan?

Kudos to those organizations who have turned their planning processes into plans that truly guide corporate decision making and provide daily direction for board and staff actions. But what about those plans sitting on office shelves?

> **"In preparing for battle I have always found that plans are useless, but planning is indispensable."**
> — **Dwight Eisenhower**

Some are beautifully and skillfully crafted, well-researched documents that have been developed with a great deal of input from all possible stakeholders. Why is it that sometimes no one ever sees those pages again? Why does it often seem that after such a plan, everything goes back to the way it always was? Why is it that we don't regularly see measurable change in an organization as a result of that plan? Why is it not a guide for daily action?

There are a number of reasons this seems to happen so often. Some have to do with the Planning and some have to do with the Plan.

When Planning Becomes a Noun

As we mentioned earlier, planning is a verb. Effective planning involves the planners in action purposely directed toward realizing and living out the values. (We will see later that the values we are referring to are bigger than the organization's values.) When strategic planning is a routine, requirement or ritual, it becomes a noun. By definition, it is not an action word. It has no life of its own. The focus is on the event of planning.

When planning is a noun, the participants become players in a theater production – acting out predetermined roles with a predetermined end that has no real meaning – a theater of the absurd, if you will. The "director" controls the output if not the outcome.

Planning must be a living, dynamic process. To use the theater metaphor, it must be an "improv" performance, growing out of the interaction between history, participants, and circumstances. The "director" uses only the values to guide the action and the outcome is a result of synergy, talent and creativity producing what no one could have predicted.

The outcome, then, is a richer, living document that is shaped by and shapes the passions of the participants.

<u>Examine your last strategic plan. Was it pre-scripted or was it allowed to evolve?</u>

When Planning is too Self-Reliant

Another reason plans are often abandoned is that the planning violates the Reliance Factor. Planning must involve The Spirit. Yes, we are referring to the Holy Spirit (with upper case letters), but even if you're not "down with that," planning must be spirit-filled (with lower case letters). That is, planning must be driven by something deeper and more mature than our own self-reliant, conscious competence. To be truly effective, we must recognize there is something more than our intellect and skills and excellent staff and board needed in our planning. We must recognize that our organization is only a part of something much bigger – something we cannot fully grasp. We must see ourselves as part of a global community, and see our staff and board and customers as complex physical, emotional and spiritual beings. Who can speak for such a large constituency? How can we gather stakeholders from such an undefined universe?

We believe the answer is the Holy Spirit and we will explain more about that later. But for now, does it not make sense that most plans sit on shelves because they are not truly relevant to reality? And is it not illogical to believe that we alone have a comprehensive understanding of such a large reality?

Examine your last strategic plan. On whose competence did you rely for its relevance?

When Planning Creates Hopelessness

Another reason plans fail to produce actionable results is that the very act of planning creates an environment of hopelessness rather than hope. Hope is a necessary prerequisite to action. When people see situations as hopeless, they become disengaged, even paralyzed. How does this hopelessness, disengagement and paralysis happen?

The widely accepted and established planning process involves a discipline called a SWOT analysis. The letters stand for Strengths, Weaknesses, Opportunities and Threats. Strengths and Weaknesses are usually internal to the organization and Opportunities and Threats are usually external. The planners chronicle all the organization's internal characteristics and then try to employ the strengths to counter or overcome the weaknesses. Likewise, they research the external environment, and attempt to exercise the strengths to make maximum use of the opportunities and to minimize the threats.

This method is also subject to the Reliance Factor – the participants must have full confidence in the organization and its strengths and must fully believe that the threats can be overcome. They must be convinced that the internal weaknesses will not disqualify them from taking advantage of the opportunities that are ahead before the competition snaps them up.

In order for hope to be the driver, the participants must have been constantly built up and equipped for success. They must be confident that those upon whom they are relying are "conquerors" and "top dogs" in their sphere of influence. And that belief must prevail both individually and corporately. In Chapter 7 we will offer an alternative to SWOT analysis that builds confidence and focuses on success, increasing hope in administration and staff.

<u>Examine your last strategic plan. Does it project an assurance of success?</u>

When the Plan Becomes the End

All too often we have seen business owners and administrators create a plan because it was a requirement from a third party – a bank, an investor or a foundation. When their purpose is simply to create a plan, it is doomed to a life on a shelf. The lesson here is to use the requirement as an opportunity to enter into a truly spirit-led planning process. Those third parties don't want a plan so that they have an extra book to put on their shelves. They are trying to engage you in an activity that is proven to bring more success.

Consider the Effort/Effect Factor here. If you and your staff see the effect as merely meeting a requirement, the effort you put in will be minimal. But even if you find yourself working very hard, you will be working toward the wrong end. Adjust your perception of the effect and your effort will be worthwhile. This is not mere semantics. It is an important attitudinal ingredient to effective planning.

Examine your last strategic plan. Is it simply a product to meet a requirement?

When the Plan is Too Big for the Planners

There is a difference between a job well-done and a job over-done. Another reason plans fail to become meaningful guides to action is that many planners enter into the process with too much sophistication. There is such a thing as too much research. Too many goals and strategies. Too many action plans. Too many participants. Too broad a scope.

A good plan is scaled to the size and the resources of the organization. The effort must be balanced with the effect. Smaller organizations – say, under 50 employees – can't afford to focus on more than two major areas of change at a time. Spending time and effort on anything past that produces "analysis paralysis." The task is simply overwhelming. There is no clear starting point.

A planning process that is too big for the organization to handle violates the Effort/Effect Factor. In addition, it is banking on non-existent resources and therefore violating the Reliance Factor.

Examine your last strategic plan. Is it unwieldy and unrealistic?

When the Plan Has No Legs

Finally, plans that have no clear execution strategies will find usefulness only in decorating office shelves. We will talk later about naming specific action plans, persons responsible, required resources and accountable timelines. Plans that lack that level of specificity simply do not get accomplished. Participants leave the planning process feeling good about the great discussion around values, vision and mission. But within a few days they are frustrated because nothing changes. In Chapter 8 we will provide a template to assure that your plans empower people rather than frustrate them.

Examine your last strategic plan. Does it have what it takes to guide specific action?

Chapter Three

Biblical Basis and Model for Planning

By now we hope you're convinced of the necessity for planning. You've seen how the Effort/Effect and the Reliance Factors influence the inputs and outcomes of the planning

"Where there is no vision, the people perish."

— **Proverbs 29:18**

process. And you have some insight into why many plans seem to just sit on the shelf.

Before we lay out the Upside-Down model, there is one more important "back story" for you to think about. Everything we do and teach has a biblical basis. For you who are Christians, it is important that you understand the Scripture that shaped this model for Spirit-led, transformation strategic planning. We find that there are a lot of misconceptions about planning in Christian circles, especially as it relates to our understanding of faith, trusting God, being content with whatever we have, etc.

For those of you who do not share the Christian worldview, we invite you to examine this chapter for its sound concepts and ideas – regardless of their source. We believe they are universal in their value and application. You do not need to believe in God to see the wisdom in identifying the highest set of values driving your decision making. You do not need to believe in the Bible to see the practicality of planning around a long-term vision that encompasses more than your self-interests. You don't have to profess faith in Christ to see the practicality in His teachings. Like this one, they contain universally accepted principles.

> "For which one of you, when he wants to build a tower, does not first sit down and calculate the cost to see if he has enough to complete it? Otherwise, when he has laid a foundation and is not able to finish, all who observe it begin to ridicule him, saying, 'This man began to build and was not able to finish.' Or what king, when he sets out to meet another king in battle, will not first sit down and consider whether he is strong enough with ten thousand men to encounter the one coming against him with twenty thousand? Or else, while the other is still far away, he sends a delegation and asks for terms of peace." (Luke 14:28-32)

We invite Christians and non-Christians alike to join us in exploring the Biblical wisdom on planning in this chapter. It's good, common sense. And it prepares you to take the next step in Upside-Down Strategic

Planning. There are numerous examples and models of planning in the Bible, but the book of Genesis has the advantage of hosting two models which encompass the very best of planning, and the very worst. By studying these two examples, we learn a lot about God's model for planning, what is successful and sustainable, and the kind of planning that overcomes even poor execution. God's model of planning brings the creative, reproductive quality of transformation.

Planning with a Larger Purpose

The first planning model is the best of planning and is contained in the account of creation. Genesis 1, the very first book, the very first verse, announces the creation of the world. Even by the most conservative estimates, this occurred at the very least over 6000 years ago. Some scholars place it much further into the past, but the important point is that creation has been successfully sustaining itself for countless generations. It has survived wars, natural disasters, and both the well-meaning and evil-intentioned actions of mankind. It even included a contingency plan to deal with the inevitable failure of those tasked with administering the plan.

What is the key ingredient to planning that provided a framework so effective, efficient and flexible that it has endured to this very day? The answer lies in Genesis 1:2, "...and the Spirit of God was hovering over the waters." (If you're not into the Bible examples, stick with us. We'll show you the relevance in the shaded paragraphs, below).

The Holy Spirit co-created with God. He hovered over the process. That word for hovers is used in Deuteronomy 32:11 to describe the way an eagle protects its nest and prepares its chicks for flight. It is an active verb and it is clear that the Holy Spirit was active in creation. While this may seem a small point, it gains significance when we look at the role of the Holy Spirit throughout Scripture. Jesus describes His role best in John 14:26.

> But the Advocate, the Holy Spirit, whom the Father will send in my name, will teach you all things and will remind you of everything I have said to you.

A little further on, Jesus says,

> But when he, the Spirit of truth, comes, he will guide you into all the truth. He will not speak on his own; he will speak only what he hears, and he will tell you what is yet to come. He will glorify me because it is from me that he will receive what he will make known to you. All that belongs to the Father is mine. That is why I said the Spirit will receive from me what he will make known to you. (John 16:13-15)

What is the purpose of reminding us, telling us what is to come, and making things known to us? We need the help. A little further on in Genesis, we see that mankind has an assigned function with regard to all of creation.

> God created man in His own image, in the image of God He created him; male and female He created them. God blessed them; and God said to them, "Be fruitful and multiply, and fill the earth,

and subdue it; and rule over the fish of the sea and over the birds of the sky and over every living thing that moves on the earth." (Gen 1:27-28)

We were set in charge of the physical world. We were charged with expanding creation and introducing it to the perfect plans God had for it. That's a tremendous responsibility and opportunity. It suggests that we are an integral part of the creation process which continues to this day. Along with the passages about the Holy Spirit, above, we also see that we are to be co-laborers with the creator in that process. We are to fill the earth and take care of it.

This model of planning clearly has "legs," in that it is working to this very day. The Effect in the Effort/Effect Factor encompasses the entire universe. And we are invited to link our Effort with that of the Holy Spirit. Coupled with High External and High Internal Reliance, the model has clear benefits.

Holy Spirit-led Planning Benefits:

- It is planning in the name of God and to accomplish the perfect will of God for the world.
- It is a process in which we are taught all things and are guided into all truth.
- In Spirit-led planning, we are reminded of all of Jesus' teaching.
- We can be sure it is the very will of God because the Spirit will speak only what he hears from God.
- Spirit-led planning takes into account what is yet to come. Who can possibly know the future?

- This planning glorifies Jesus because the Holy Spirit makes known to us what He receives from Jesus.
- It glorifies the Father because all that Jesus gives to the Spirit is from the Father.

Now, what about someone who doesn't know or believe there is a Holy Spirit? We have used this model with secular organizations and units of government very successfully. Here's how we explain the relevance. We believe that guiding all mankind is a universal truth. While we call that "God," in the person of the Holy Spirit, most people acknowledge the existence of such a truth. When we take the time and effort to identify that (or whom) on which we ultimately rely, we are bringing that universal truth into our reckoning.

The Reliance Factor dictates that we find the highest referent power we can access in order to maximize the effectiveness of our planning. Beyond human knowledge, most people have a deep, internal awareness of a spiritual power or universal truth that they know exists.

All but the last two of the Holy Spirit-led Planning benefits, above, are all still relevant when we are guided by whatever our bottom-line reality is.

The planning model presented in Genesis and espoused by Jesus in the New Testament is perfect. The plan follows exactly the will of God, applying all truth and knowledge even to future events that we cannot otherwise know. Why would we want to use any other model? Well, just to reinforce that thought, let's look at the other model in Genesis – the one that describes the very worst of planning.

Babel Planning

> **"The intelligent have plans; the wise have principles."**
>
> — Raheel Farooq

The second model is also presented in Genesis. First, here's a little backstory. After God saved a remnant of the people of the earth through a man named Noah and his family, he blessed them and said, "Be fruitful and increase in number and fill the earth." He emphasizes the importance of the command by repeating it saying "As for you, be fruitful and increase in number; multiply on the earth and increase upon it." Sound familiar? It's the same command given in the Genesis 1 description of planning. (Genesis 9:2 and 7)

Man's Reaction Reveals the Planning Model.

"Now the whole world had one language and a common speech. As people moved eastward, they found a plain in Shinar and settled there. They said to each other, 'Come, let's make bricks and bake them thoroughly.' They used brick instead of stone, and tar for mortar. Then they said, 'Come, let us build ourselves a city, with a tower that reaches to the heavens, so that we may make a name for ourselves; otherwise we will be scattered over the face of the whole earth.

But the LORD came down to see the city and the tower the people were building. The LORD said, 'If as one people speaking the same language they have begun to do this, then nothing they plan to do will be impossible for them. Come, let us go down and confuse their language so they will not understand each other.' So the LORD scattered them from there over all the earth, and they stopped building the city. That is why it was called Babel—because there the LORD confused the language of the whole world. From there the LORD scattered them over the face of the whole earth." (Genesis 11:1-9)

Wait, this sounds like a model of good planning, commended by God Himself, saying that if they can do this, their planning can accomplish anything. But God was clearly not pleased with their accomplishment or with their planning. Here's the key sentence, (with the addition of our emphasis),

> "Then they said, 'Come, let us build *ourselves* a city, with a tower that reaches to the heavens, so that we may make a name for *ourselves*; otherwise we will be scattered over the face of the whole earth."

Their planning lands in the worst quadrants of both the Effort/Effect and the Reliance Factors. The Effect they were after fell far short of the total effect planning was to have on the whole world. They were focused on themselves and on the short term outcome of providing a name and a place for themselves. Caring for the whole world and expanding the wonders of creation throughout the earth were the furthest things from their minds.

And they were reliant completely on their own efforts. The bigger vision and mission were scrapped because they turned their backs on and even opposed the direct will of the tremendous resources they had at their disposal.

Babel Planning Has These Major Drawbacks:

- It is conceived in selfish reasons. ("...let us build ourselves a city.")
- It attempts to set mankind up as equal to God Himself. ("...tower that reaches to the heavens.")
- Its goal is to remove mankind's dependence on God. ("...that we may make a name for ourselves.")
- The desired result is to rebel against God's express command. ("...otherwise we will be scattered over the whole earth.")

Once again, for those who discount God or the Holy Spirit as the source, consider this. Does it not resonate within you, that planning to achieve selfish ends, at the expense of the larger goals of mankind, is poor planning? Is it not logical that discounting the vast knowledge and experience of "a higher power" is foolish, at best, and puts the success of the plan at risk?

So, time for a decision:

Planning using the infinite wisdom and knowledge of God, or my own mind?

Planning with an eternal, global strategy, or my own narrow agenda?

Planning in cooperation with the ultimate winner, or in rebellion with a defeated few?

Which one do you choose?

God's Promises for Transformation Planning

A few more things to help set the stage for Upside-Down Strategic Planning. God often announces His plans through covenants. Simply put, He determines and announces a long-term plan to benefit His people and promises to carry it through forever. Here are some examples:

> "To your descendants I give this land" (Genesis 15:18)

> "I will give… an everlasting possession to you and your descendants after you; and I will be their God." (Genesis 17:8)

> "He and his descendants will have a covenant of a lasting priesthood." (Numbers 25:13)

> "And I will establish the throne of his kingdom forever." (2 Samuel 7:13)

> "I will put my law in their minds and write it on their hearts…I will forgive their wickedness and remember their sins no more." (Jeremiah 31:33; 34)

God did not, however make these strategic plans binding on us. He gives us free will and the right to opt out if we don't want the benefits. If we choose to opt out, we lose the guarantee except by His mercy and grace. Many times throughout history, the Israelites "opted out" of their side – committing themselves to God and to His ways. The result was that they spent as much or more time outside the Promised Land than inside. Individual priests "opted out" and were cut down in the prime of their lives without ever seeing the promises come true.

He has made the Effect (the outcome) clear. And He has defined the Effort He expects from us, which is High Reliance on Him.

A fair summary of this whole discussion on Spirit-led strategic planning is this: Reliance on God – which the Bible calls "resting in Him" and "obedience," results in **God's** plans for us. "Self-reliance," "resting on our own plans and efforts" or "disobedience," results in **our** plans for us. And we've already determined which are better.

Our Part in Transformation Planning

So far, our focus has been on God doing the planning. How does that relate to a Kingdom company or organization making plans for a strategic transformation of an industry, a market, or a city? God's plan all along has been to give us the authority to make plans and the power to carry them out. In Genesis 1, "God blessed them [Adam and Eve] and said to them, 'Be fruitful and increase in number; fill the earth and subdue it. Rule over the fish in the sea and the birds in the sky and over every living creature that moves on the ground.'" Yet eventually, man and woman abdicated their position as strategic co-planners with God. By willfully stepping out of His will for them, they chose to try to make their own way. The result? Well, you can see for yourself the shape the world is in.

God, however, had contingencies built into His eternal strategic plan. He sent His Son, Jesus, who came, "to seek and to save that which was lost." (Luke 19:10) He handed back to us the keys to the Kingdom we had relinquished.

> "I will give you the keys of the kingdom of heaven; whatever you bind on earth will be bound in heaven, and whatever you loose on earth will be loosed in heaven." (Matthew 16:19)

He set us up as His agents to co-labor with Him to reclaim the entire earth.

> "Then Jesus came to them and said, 'All authority in heaven and on earth has been given to me. Therefore go and make disciples of all nations, baptizing them in the name of the Father and of the Son and of the Holy Spirit, and teaching them to obey everything I have commanded you. And surely I am with you always, to the very end of the age.' " (Matthew 28:18-19)

Ephesians 1:9-10 tells us that God has put His strategic plan back on track through us:

> "He made known to us the mystery of his will according to his good pleasure, which he purposed in Christ, to be put into effect when the times reach their fulfillment--to bring unity to all things in heaven and on earth under Christ. (Ephesians 1:9-10 NIV)

Once again, we find ourselves with a charge to steward all creation.

How are we to accomplish such a mammoth task? Most organizational strategic plans have a section listing resources and responsible parties. God's plan has no less of an equipping strategy. That strategy was quoted in the two passages from John 14 and 16 at the beginning of this chapter. Jesus sets the task and the Holy Spirit equips us for it. He is the enabler. He is the person designated to prepare and monitor us in the planning and execution process.

> "Christ himself gave the apostles, the prophets, the evangelists, the pastors and teachers, to equip his people for works of service, so that the body of Christ may be built up until we all reach unity in the faith and in the knowledge of the Son of God and become mature, attaining to the whole measure of the fullness of Christ." (Ephesians 4:11-13)

> "Now to each one the manifestation of the Spirit is given for the common good." (1 Corinthians 12:7)

How does someone who does not credit God as the creator receive these thoughts? That depends completely on how you view the world and your place in it. Are you an insignificant speck in the primordial soup of the universe, or do you hold and exercise influence over your world? If you see yourself with the first belief, then we have to challenge why you are even reading a book on planning. But if you at least see humans as having some hierarchical control over how events and circumstances affect your future, then the concepts above translate like this.

There is a preferred, beneficial future for mankind and we here on this earth are endowed with intelligence, strength and authority to shape that future. Our attitude about the greater good, the universal truth, and a higher power puts us in a unique position to proactively build a legacy that will carry into future generations, equipping them for a successful life. Our reliance on that attitude imbues us with power and authority and enables us to put in all the Effort needed to produce the Effect. See Appendix 2 for more.

The Holy Spirit in Planning

That last passage goes on to talk in depth about the "manifestation" of the Holy Spirit in terms of supernatural gifts, which working together with the gifts other believers have, creates the comprehensive approach to strategic planning that we describe below. To prepare for that, let's look briefly at the person of the Holy Spirit and the area of spiritual gifts. Such a study is beyond the scope of this book, but we would be irresponsible if we didn't mention a few things here.

The Holy Spirit is a person – one of the three persons of the Trinity and as such is as alive and real as God the Father and God the Son. His work in creation, throughout the Old and New Testaments, and in our hearts today is readily discernible. The subject makes some people uncomfortable, though. We want to make sure you understand how important it is for you to acknowledge and accept the Holy Spirit's participation in your life. The scriptures we introduced in this chapter make it clear that a relationship with Him is invaluable. If you are lacking teaching in this area, or if you have been taught that the Holy Spirit and His gifts were only meant for the times of the early church, please ask God to personally give you wisdom and knowledge in this area. Take out your Bible and do a word study on spirit and Holy Spirit and see what you find. Get a couple study guides from a Christian bookstore and work through them. Seek out other believers who are comfortable in this area and talk with them. We also have a free teaching available from Greater Works Ministries On-line Healing School.

http://www.greaterworksministries.us/teachings/

Once you are convinced of the importance of the person and gifts of the Holy Spirit, begin the process of learning about the area(s) in which you have been gifted. We believe that you will find both personal and corporate areas of giftedness, i.e., you yourself operate in certain gifts and there is also a collection of gifts among your staff and leaders, that when taken together provide a well-rounded ability to perform supernaturally in the natural world.

2 Timothy 1:6 has Paul reminding Timothy "to fan into flame the gift of God," which suggests that we can learn and grow within our areas of giftedness. Let this be a regular, ongoing part of your preparation for Upside-Down strategic planning.

Finally, to wrap up this discussion for those who have been trusting us to supply some rationale other than a Biblical view, we suggest you simply look around you. It is immediately apparent that some people are highly gifted. It has been proven in research over the years that there is a giftedness that comes from "nature" rather than "nurture." How you believe those extraordinary gifts are given does not change the fact that they exist and that we have a responsibility to use those gifts for the greater good.

Chapter Four

The Upside-Down approach - Values First

Traditional planning begins with identifying the mission and vision. These come out of the heart of the founder(s). The organization's values, then, are stated

Our Mission

Our Vision

Our Values

— **Traditional Model**

in support of that mission and vision. Though that model starts with "our mission," it is actually seated in the values we hold that have given rise to our mission. Something inside of us has driven us to define our mission. Perhaps it is something deep and abiding, like our love for the environment. Perhaps it is something less lofty, like our need to accumulate wealth. But make no mistake about it – behind every mission there is a set of values.

The limiting factor here, is that our values, as admirable as they may be, are tainted by our life experiences, our peer group, our culture and our personal attitudes and beliefs. None of us is perfect. Whether by nature or nurture, we have been shaped by the world with all its limitations.

Though it has worked well for decades, the mission/vision/values model falls short of the "higher order" planning described in the last chapter. As carefully as the planners may try to take into account the greater good, they will still be basing their mission on their own misguided values, shaped by their limited understanding and world viewpoint. They will miss the greatest good that comes from the pure motives of God and His perfect will for us. Unless planning is grounded in the highest values, the universal truth, the cosmic awareness, it will by definition be limited in its effectiveness and in its reach.

From here on, when we refer to Holy-Spirit planning, we'll trust that those of you who need to, will make the connection to whatever it is that you see as the broader, deeper Reliance Factor described in Chapter 2 and as explained in Chapter 3. You can supply the words you are more comfortable with yourself.

These next three chapters will walk you through the Values/Vision/Mission portion of the Upside-Down Strategic Planning model. In a nutshell you will be asking and answering three questions:

What are God's values?

If all of those values were in place, what would our sphere of influence look like? That is, what is God's vision?

What part do we play in realizing that vision? That is, what is our mission?

God's Values as the Basis for Planning

The fundamental question in Spirit-led strategic planning is, "Whose values do we serve?" What defines the vision of the future? To be truly Spirit-led, both of these must originate with a clear discerning of God's values and vision and our willingness to hear and obey His direction for us – our mission.

God's Values

God's Vision

Our Mission

— **Spirit-Led Model**

In our consulting, we spend a great deal of time and effort in examining Personal and Corporate Purity, to be sure the organization is unerringly focused on God's agenda. We try to eliminate everything which could be an impediment to hearing and obeying the call of God on our lives and on our organizations. We try to cleanse ourselves and our businesses from that which would prevent us from being a clear conduit through which God's plans and purposes will flow. Visit our website for more on Personal and Corporate Purity.

http://www.market70.com/index.php/step-2-purity/attain-and-protect-purity

For both secular and Christian organizations we walk through the same process, trying to identify anything in their past or present which could impede their ability to identify and serve the greater good. These might include hidden agendas of owners, ties to immoral or criminal activities, unethical practices, conflicts of interests and the like.

It is vital that we recognize the immense impact any activity can have if it syncs with and molds itself to God's values, vision and mission – a transformational view of its participation in attaining the greatest good. This means that any activity we are involved in – our great-grandfather's appliance repair shop, the 75 year-old social service organization we are on the board of, or the city council we sit on or the business we plan to incorporate next month – must seek God's values and vision in order to be a truly Spirit-led, transformation business.

So, step one of the Upside-Down Strategic Planning Model begins with an ongoing, intense listening process to hear what His values are. It begins not with mission and vision, but with values – His values. It is imperative that we really press into what God's heart is in terms of – you fill in the blanks – His product, His service, His employees, His customers, etc. Knowing, understanding and fully accepting His values may completely change the way you conduct your activities.

In Luke 19, we hear Jesus telling the parable about the ruler who goes off to get himself crowned as king of the territory. Before he leaves he gathers ten of his servants and entrusts each of them with a sum of money, instructing them to "do business" with it until he returns. We all know the story: one multiplies the money ten-fold, another returns five-fold on the investment and one buries the money and returns only the principle. Of the three, only the first two seemed to know and understand that the ruler had a broader mission than simply to turn a profit. From his comments on returning, his mission was at least in part to prepare his kingdom and equip his servants to effectively rule. Had the third servant understood and accepted that mission, he would have handled the assignment very differently.

How did those first two know the ruler's values? We aren't told, but we can surmise that they must have watched the ruler closely over time. They must have paid attention to how he governed, how he used his resources. They must have become familiar with his character. They must have asked questions when they were given assignments so that they understood why he was directing them as he was. They must have looked over the history of his territory and the part he played in building it into what it was.

We know they must have gotten it right because when he returned he was so pleased with how they handled his affairs while he was gone that he put them in charge of cities. They went from being servants to being governors. They had demonstrated to him that they shared his values, and therefore he could trust them to govern in his name.

A Real Illustration of Discovering God's Values

One of our previous businesses, About Purpose, Inc. can serve as an illustration. Since 1985, the mission ("my" mission) had been from Colossians 2:2-3 – "My goal is that they may be encouraged in heart and united in love, so that they may have the full riches of complete understanding, in order that they may know the mystery of God, namely, Christ, in whom are hidden all the treasures of wisdom and knowledge." How could I possibly go wrong? The mission was directly out of God's Word!

Then as we entered into Spirit-led Strategic Planning, we immersed ourselves in understanding God's values – His heart for the marketplace, the priority He places on nations and not just individuals, and His unchanging desire to establish us as co-laborers in His creation. We started with Scripture and studied what God said about having dominion over creation, spreading throughout the world, increasing and multiplying. We read the numerous passages around how he values quality work and work done for his glory.

We saw more deeply into Christ's work and what He was called to do. We realized that it is God's will that we model ourselves after Jesus. As God sent Jesus into the world, so Jesus sends us. (John 20:21) We saw Jesus bringing a Kingdom gospel that was much broader than personally knowing Him and accepting Him as Savior. (Luke 4:18-19)

We began asking questions that reveal His values around the world of consulting and training in which He had placed us. And we began writing down answers as we heard them.

Q. "What does God care about in this area?"

A. He clearly values education, knowledge and wisdom as evidenced throughout both the Old and New Testaments. He has spoken often about all three, explicitly as well as implicitly.

A. His plan has always been to send people out to carry His Word and carry on His work. He made that clear in Genesis 1:26 and 28 and repeated that value numerous time throughout Scripture. Jesus confirmed the importance of that value in what we call The Great Commission (Matthew 28:18-20); and in the account from which we get our current corporate name, Market 70 International. (Luke 10:1-9)

A. From that same passage and numerous others throughout recorded history, we know that He values nations and people groups and desires that His plans and purposes for them are communicated to them and that they are equipped to step into them.

A. Because He has gifted people as teachers, apostles, evangelists, pastors and prophets for the equipping of His church, we know He values the use of those gifts and the building up of His people (Ephesians 4:11-13).

Q. "What makes God weep? If He were human, what would keep Him up at night?"

A. The only instance in which we see Jesus literally weeping is in Luke 19:41-44 when he foresaw the destruction of Jerusalem, showing a heart for cities.

A. But in several places we also see Him "deeply moved in spirit and…troubled" when He sees the suffering of loved ones who had suffered a premature death in their family.

A. We know that he highly values good leadership. He felt compassion for people who were distressed and lacking leadership. He spoke about Himself being "The Good Shepherd." And God continually rebuked the leaders of the Israelites for not taking care of the people.

A. He also felt compassion for those who were sick (Matthew 9:36 and 14:14), for those who were hungry (Matthew 15:32), and for those who had lost their way (Luke 15:11-32). Does this not show His heart and what He cares about?

Q. "What delights God?"

A. We see throughout Scripture that He delights in those who obey the voice of the Lord (1 Samuel, 15:22) and He doesn't delight in empty gestures of love and obedience.

A. He highly values those who are righteous or upright (Proverbs 21:3), as can be seen throughout Psalms and Proverbs. See especially Proverbs 11:10 which gives further insight into why He delights in the righteous. That passage leads us to see that He values those who use the fruit of their righteousness to benefit His cities and His people.

Q. "Who are the kinds of people He Himself called 'blessed'?"

A. The answers we found to this question really helped us see what some of His values are. We noted those that we felt have something to do with the area of work to which He had called us. Those who are blessed are those who...

- have obeyed My voice (Genesis 22:18)

- do not walk in the counsel of the wicked (Psalm 1:1)

- consider the helpless (Psalm 41:1)

- those who keep justice, who practice righteousness at all times (Psalm 106:3)

- find wisdom and who gain understanding (Proverbs 3:13)

- sow beside all waters and let out freely the ox and the donkey (In Isaiah 32:20 and elsewhere, Isaiah speaks to the importance of investing in community building and spreading the wealth.)

And...

- blessed is the nation whose God is the LORD (Psalm 33:12)

- blessed is the man whose strength is in You (Psalm 84:5)

- blessed are you, O land, whose king is of nobility and whose princes eat at the appropriate time—for strength and not for drunkenness.

- blessed are the peacemakers, for they shall be called sons of God (Matthew 5:9)

Are you beginning to see how we can discern the values of God from what He says in the Bible? We were impressed with His heart for the disenfranchised and those who seek to help them. We saw the high regard He placed on righteous leaders in both spiritual and secular realms. We saw His desire that people learn and walk in their identity as co-laborers with Him.

In addition to Scripture, we chronicled what He had been doing in our own lives – preparing and equipping us with gifts and opportunities. We asked ourselves why He had shaped us as He had, why He had exposed us to certain events and situations, and why He had called us to do and learn certain things throughout our lives.

We began to see that what was important to God in this area of consulting and training was much bigger than the mission we had chosen. Our mission was just one part of what God wanted us to embrace. As we heard His heart, we saw that He was leading us into something much bigger, and yet much narrower at the same time.

What Values Does He Hold Dear in Your Area?

"Well, that's easy for you. You are a Christian organization," you might say. But you will find values in every sphere. How will you go about discerning what's on God's heart in the area He has you working? Here are some practical ideas for you in hearing Him in this area. We recommend you pull together some trusted colleagues who have an understanding of whatever you see your mission as. It doesn't matter if they are Christians, although if yours is a Christian organization you will certainly want to include spiritually mature colleagues.

Note that these steps will overlap, but we recommend you go through them all. Each will bring a slightly different perspective and each will get you thinking about what's really important in the bigger scheme of things.

Hear Specifically

This first step is one that is useful through all the remaining steps. When we ask people to begin naming values, the tendency is to name general, rather undefined terms: honesty, integrity, love, trust, etc. There is no doubt these are important and fundamental values, but what do they mean? We ask people to put values into behavioral term. Rather than a word – honesty – you will write a description. "We value honesty, that characteristic that people demonstrate over time; that they can be trusted with money and account information in a way that is both transparent and reliable; that they consistently show the same degree of care for our resources as do the owners of the company."

As people name a value, ask them, "What does honesty look like in our sphere, our industry, our culture, etc.?" This will lead to rich discussion that reveals fundamental beliefs. The participants will begin to make those values real and in so doing they will also begin to own them. One of the ancient Greek philosophers once said, "The teaching of virtue [values] is the asking of questions." People's values solidify as they talk about them, hold them up to real situations, and challenge others' interpretations of them.

One time we were working with a county mental health agency and asking them to name the values that they believed were most basic and important to their work. They began talking about access to health care and we challenged them to describe that in behavioral terms, i.e., what would that look like in their county? What followed was a lively discussion that ended up identifying many other values around funding, personal choice of providers, freedom to choose one's level and speed of recovery and degree of reentry, etc. When we got around to redefining mission, there was a very different and deeper understanding of providing mental health care in the county.

Hear from Scripture

This is an excellent source of identifying values. Even non-believers recognize the strong benefit of most of the Bible's values to individuals and society.

The process is not as easy as one might think, though. You can't simply look up "trust" in the concordance (an index most Bibles have that lists the major words and themes and where to find them). You need to read and understand the accounts of people's struggle to trust God, of individuals who demonstrated trust, of the nations who violated both human and divine trust, and of the character of God Himself as trustworthy.

One danger to be aware of is "proof-texting." If you want to, you can probably find a passage that either proves or disproves almost anything. It's important to have people on your team that are very familiar with Scripture, so that they can help interpret the meaning of the stories of God's people, and who can provide the knowledge of how a particular value or belief might be treated throughout all of Scripture.

Hear from the Holy Spirit

Scripture is referred to in Greek as *logos*, or the spoken word of God, meaning that it has been heard and recorded. There is another Greek word, *rhema*, which refers to the current or ongoing word of God.

Christians familiar with *rhema* understand it to be what we hear from the Holy Spirit as we described in Chapter 3. He is available to us to teach us, guide us and counsel us.

> "I will ask the Father, and He will give you another Helper, that He may be with you forever; that is the Spirit of truth, whom the world cannot receive, because it does not see Him or know Him, but you know Him because He abides with you and will be in you. ... But the Helper, the Holy Spirit, whom the Father will send in My name, He will teach you all things, and bring to your remembrance all that I said to you. (John 14:16-17, 26)

This passage is talking about revelation. His *rhema* voice includes His speaking to us in His Word, through other people, through dreams, visions, and inner impressions, through words of knowledge or wisdom or prophesy. Has God spoken to you in any of these ways? Write them down, or if you have already, go back and look and pray over them to see if there are trends or repetition.

Ask God to speak to you now – fresh and new for today. Ask your intercessors* to query the Lord on your behalf as well, and to ready your heart to hear His heart. Expect to hear Him. James 1:5-8 tells us that when we ask for wisdom (a word from God) we must believe that we have received it. Listen. Write down what you hear – even if it doesn't appear to be from God. You can sort it all out later. Trust that He has answered your request for a fresh word. He may lead you to a Scripture passage. He may remind you of a sermon or a song. He may give you a dream.

People from some cultures regularly receive revelation through visions and dreams. Know this: He will reveal Himself to you.

*In our consulting, we recommend every organization and every leader have a team of intercessors – people whose calling is to hold you and your mission up in prayer and to intentionally listen to the Holy Spirit's guidance on your behalf. During this time of trying to identify God's values for your organization, it would be good to have this team operating behind the scenes and adding what they hear to what you are hearing. For more on intercession, visit that portion of our website.

http://www.market70.com/index.php/step-1-intercession/your-intercessory-team

Hear from Experiences

Looking at your own life and the history of your organization will reveal some of your deeply held values. It is important to discuss these and question whether they are values that are consistent with what you really believe. For example, one non-profit we worked with had a successful history of bringing prisoners into a life with Christ. But as they talked about it they realized they were disappointed in their work. So many of the prisoners finished their sentences and found they had nothing to go back to. Their families were broken, their communities no longer trusted them, many had no skills to get good jobs, etc. This discussion revealed for them that while their work was consistent with their value on a relationship with Christ, it didn't include carrying that out in relationship with family, community, workplace, etc. This realization impacted their mission greatly and expanded it to something much bigger and much more successful.

Ask God to show you how you got to where you are now. Highlight the events in your life, and later, in your business, that have formed you. Where do you see His hand? What has He been trying to teach you? Were there points at which He seemed to open or close doors that you didn't expect? Who are the significant people that He brought into your path and what effect did they have on you? Were there times in your life when you felt his rebuke at a course of action you were taking or failing to take?

Now, summarize what He has been building into you. Put into words the things He has been showing you are important to Him in your life and development. These are His values.

Another, related way to glean God's values from your own experiences is to look at your gifts and talents. Do you know what your God-given gifts are? Identify your natural gifts - those He gave to you through your personality, character, upbringing, schooling, experiences, etc. What are those things you have a passion for, those things that drive you and those things that bring you to tears? Now, identify your supernatural gifts – those given you by the Holy Spirit for specific times, places or ministries, for the building up of the body of Christ. (If you don't know your gifts – either your natural or your supernatural – it might be wise for you to pause in the process and learn about this area. Take a gift inventory – one that measures both the natural and supernatural. Ask your spiritual advisor, pastor, or intercessors to help you in this step.)

Many teach that where you see an intersection between your natural gifts and your passion, you are looking at what is important to God – His values. If you also see the operation of supernatural gifts in that calling, you can be sure you have is highlighting His values for the vision He has in mind for you.

Hear from Others

This step recognizes a part of that Reliance Factor we talked about in Chapter 2. There are experts in your field that it would be wise to listen to. What beliefs do they espouse? What values do they demonstrate? What are the dominant values in the culture in which you operate?

We purposely put this as the last step because we feel it is important that you have first listened to God's heart through Scripture, the Holy Spirit and through your own experiences. It may be that your discernment of values will be affirmed. It may be that you are being called to hold up different interpretation of values than those being modeled in your sphere of influence. It may even be that you are called to challenge them and to put forth opposing values.

As you discuss the beliefs of others and that of your industry, culture, etc., you will, by this time have internalized the values that are on God's heart. You may experience a "cognitive dissonance," an uneasy sense or outright realization that what you hold dear is not what is being practiced. This may be the beginning of a paradigm shift, in which you recognize that "the way we always do things" is no longer the right thing or the most effective thing.

An example of this is how the whole approach to charitable giving is changing. Some of the biggest aid organizations in the world are being challenged to look at the unintended consequences of their donations as a result of discovering different values and beliefs to guide philanthropy that create development and growth rather than entropy and dependence.

Your task is to clearly list out the values that you and your team have heard. The values will be stated in terms of beliefs or importance or passion. Here is an example of values one group working to improve parenting identified: a love for children, outrage at injustice, God's longing for intimacy with His children, a desire to disciple or train others, a passion to see problems solved and distractions removed, etc. They wrote, "God is disappointed when He sees kids wasting their young lives; when He sees parents unable to pass on any sense of relevancy to their kids. He's saddened by parents who can't relate to their children; who don't know how to communicate with them and are afraid to try because of their own inadequacies."

(Can you see all of these values in Scripture? Search deeply all that God says not only about parents and children as a topic, but what He says about HIS children, their identity and how He wants them to relate to Him).

The next pages contain a summary of our suggestions for walking you and your staff through the process of hearing and recording God's values for you and your organization in your sphere of influence. Once you've accomplished this you are ready to move onto the next, even more exciting, thought and action-provoking steps: seeing God's vision for the future and for the here and now.

Identifying God's Values

Implementation Suggestions

1.   Create an event

Set aside time. We suggest at least two hours – more if you have no one who can facilitate and guide you along while capturing and naming the values from your discussion.

Invite people who are passionate and know about the sphere of influence in which you work. Don't involve so many people that it becomes unwieldy.

Include someone who is familiar with scripture who can help direct the group in identifying passages that speak to the ideas they are hearing.

2.   Set the Stage

Either have the participants read this chapter ahead of time, or take the opportunity to relate the importance and essence of hearing God's values.

If you or your participants do not share the Christian viewpoint from which this is written, be sure you discuss the "universal" ideas and truths presented.

3.   Ask questions and Listen to What's Underneath the Answers

Questions we find useful include:

What does God like or dislike around this area in which we work? What delights Him and what might make Him cry?

What are the fundamental beliefs that underlie our involvement in this area? (Especially useful for secular participants and organizations.

What is God's character and how does it relate to our clients, products or services?

Who are the "heroes" in our field and why do we hold them in high esteem?

4.   Record the Answers

If you have a bigger group, try starting with everyone writing what they're hearing on Post It notes and stick them up around the room. Then you can begin reading them aloud and collecting them into groups of similar values.

To the extent that you can, record the sources from which you draw the values. It may be several Bible passages, or research of best practices, or a word of knowledge from one of your intercessors.

5.   Prepare the Final List of Values

While we say, "final," we find that during the visioning step, we often refine the list and add or combine values. During that next step, make sure that each participant has a copy or that one in large print is prominently displayed.

If you are a secular organization using Biblical values, you may want to prepare two lists – one for public consumption and one for the planning team. The public list may be rewritten so that the meaning of the values are clear to everyone without the Scriptural language. (Appendix One contains a suggested format for listing out the values).

Chapter Five

The Upside-Down approach – God's Vision

Let's review where you are now in the Upside-Down Strategic Planning Process. You prepared ourselves to sit down and hear God's values in the sphere in which He has you working. You learned what's important to Him, what He holds dear and even what He wants you to steer away from. You came up with a list of values, expressed in behavioral language.

The next step is to ask a question that will position you and your team to hear God's vision.

Given these things that define what is important and what is foundational to the greatest good, what would your area of operations look like if every one of those values were actually in place? What would be the ideal in your sphere of influence?

The answer, of course, is perfection.

Let's revisit our example of the nonprofit agency working in the prison industry, whom we introduced in the last chapter. They posed this question based on the values they heard.

Since...

"God sacrificed His Son so that each one of those prisoners could freely and wholly enter into His family. More than that, He makes His intention clear that the prisoners would be freed – not only from the jail cells, but from those things which resulted in their being imprisoned. He wills that their eyes, blinded by the evil and selfishness in this world, would be opened. He desires that they be good fathers to their children and husbands to their wives. He values their work as sacred and as a vital contribution to the building of the now and future Kingdom here on earth. He values their actively contributing to the work of spreading the good news of that kind of freedom and purpose to everyone they meet. He expects that everyone in the community would be reaching out in love to those prisoners and their families, creating a way for them to be wholly reintegrated as valued members of their churches, business and social groups. He eagerly desires that they know and walk in their identity as those He has chosen to be His beloved sons."

Then...

"What would it look like if all those things God so cherishes were actually in operation? What is His vision for the men, families and communities of those currently in correctional institutions?"

From that question, they began to describe God's vision. I no longer have the notes from that meeting, but the vision statement, as it unfolded, took on a form something like this.

"In all 87 counties of Minnesota, community members are actively involved in eliminating the stigma and negative effects of incarceration. Churches are coordinating cooperation between government, business and education to create an environment in which prisoners' families are thriving while their loved ones are in prison and they are receiving everything they need to prepare their homes for the released men's reentry. In the jails, men are actively involved in preparing themselves spiritually, socially, emotionally, physically and economically to live full and productive lives upon their release. They understand and accept their identity as co-laborers with God in the reclamation not only of their own lives, but of the families, communities and even the country which have been damaged by the criminal activity of which they had been a part."

> **Then I saw a new heaven and a new earth, for the first heaven and the first earth had passed away, and there was no longer any sea. I saw the Holy City, the New Jerusalem**
>
> — **Revelation 21:1-2**

What a vision! It is a vision that depicts a future that is shaped by the values they had heard. Notice it is expressed in the present tense. God sees things that are not as though they are (Romans 4:17). Stating the vision in the present tense helps you, your employees, and all your constituents think of it as a reality rather than a dream. It instills a living hope into what you are doing because it describes the outcome of your efforts as a sure thing.

The group working with parenting we described above wrote out the vision they drew from the values like this. "We see kids and parents in meaningful conversations with each other throughout the day. We see parents who have the skills, knowledge and tools to interact with their kids in a way the kids can respect and look forward to. We see communication barriers created by the time demands on both kids and their parents broken down and made irrelevant."

How much more would that group be energized by such a vision, than by an abstract description of the problem of poor parenting causing problems among our youth? A well-conceived, beautifully-written vision is one of the keys to helping ourselves and others to "own" the future. It is the difference between the impossible task of trying to motivate people and the highly successful method of providing the environment in which people will motivate themselves.

Much has been written about vision, visioning, and vision-casting – all confirming the importance of holding a clear and compelling vision out for all to ascribe to. In his *Seven Habits of Highly Effective People,* Stephen Covey encouraged his readers to "Begin with the end in mind." We agree completely, but we think it is equally important to know the beginnings of the end. Without "value, valuing and value-casting" the vision can completely misguide us. The familiar story of the person climbing the ladder to success, only to find it is leaning against the wrong building, is a good warning. A vision is only as good as the values that give birth to it.

As we have seen, a vision that is built on God's values is one that is grounded in God's good and perfect will for us and all of mankind (Romans 12:2). This is the universal truth, the overriding good. A vision that calls us to anything else, no matter how compelling and well-written, will still fall short. Vision must call us to the highest of values.

This is why the traditional model is inadequate. We cannot envision a future and then conjure up values to support it. That's the equivalent of the old saying, "It's easier to ask forgiveness than to ask permission." It is terribly risky to act and then ask a blessing on our actions. It leads to an organizational anarchy in which employees or volunteers do whatever they think is right. Both common sense and Scripture convinces us that even the best-intentioned people can't have a complete picture of what's best.

"Most of the evil in this world is done by people with good intentions." (T.S. Eliot)

"Real knowledge is to know the extent of one's ignorance." (Confucius)

"No man's knowledge here can go beyond his experience." (John Locke)

"The learning and knowledge that we have, is, at the most, but little compared with that of which we are ignorant." (Plato)

"There is a way which seems right to a man, but its end is the way of death." (Proverbs 14:12)

"For My thoughts are not your thoughts, nor are your ways My ways," declares the LORD. "For as the heavens are higher than the earth, so are My ways higher than your ways and My thoughts than your thoughts." (Isaiah 55:8-9)

Time spent on identifying and "owning" the underlying truth is time well spent. When we intentionally craft a vision from those values we can be assured that the outcome that follows will be grounded in the highest of values.

Another reason for this upside-down approach is so that the vision will be complete. Crafting a vision from our own knowledge and experience and passion will probably result in a future that falls far short of what it could be. Either it will be missing some key values that are vital to the ideal future, and/or it will fall prey to unintended consequences because it failed to take into account the entire spectrum of values necessary for excellence in outcome.

An example of this shortcoming comes from the Christian Church. In her book, *Kingdom Calling: Vocational Stewardship for the Common Good*, Amy Sherman points out two places in which Christians miss the total picture of God's vision. She says we have too narrow a view of the gospel and an inadequate view of heaven. In the former, Christians have understood God's vision for salvation of the world as only saving individual souls. Christ Himself laid out a much bigger vision:

> "The Spirit of the Lord is upon me, because he anointed me to preach the gospel to the poor. He has sent me to proclaim release to the captives, and recovery of sight to the blind, to set free those who are oppressed, to proclaim the favorable year of the Lord." (Luke 4:18-19)

Because we have seen the vision of the gospel too narrowly, we have missed the call to restore the world as laid out in Isaiah 61 from which Jesus quotes His mission. Although individual transformation is vital, we have erred in focusing all our attention on individuals. Jesus sends us to disciple nations.

Likewise, Sherman points out our inadequate view of heaven. The broadly accepted view of heaven is a place somewhere in space, in which the faithful in disembodied, spiritual form will float around singing praises to God all day and all night. The unintended consequence of that other worldly view is that Christians fail to understand either their worth or their mission on this earth, both now and in eternity.

> "I saw the Holy City, the New Jerusalem...The nations will walk by its light, and the kings of the earth will bring their splendor into it. On no day will its gates ever be shut, for there will be no night there. The glory and honor of the nations will be brought into it." (Revelation 21:24-26)

Understanding the fullness of God's value on His creation leads to the truth that heaven, the Kingdom of God, is established here, on earth. Therefore, our mission here includes a stewardship meant to rebuild this world, preparing it for the fullness of the reign of the Eternal King. This realization of our calling and our worth shapes a quite different view of our identity, which is, at least to me, far more exciting than picturing myself in the midst of harps and baby angels.

The upside-down, values-first vision is necessary to focus us on a future that is solidly grounded in what's important. A vision based on values assures us that what we are working toward is worth working toward.

If It Ain't Writ, It Ain't Done

I once had a teacher that drilled into us this truth (admittedly ungrammatical): if a vision is only in your mind, then it isn't a true vision. Writing the vision down serves some very important functions.

> **Then the LORD answered me and said, "Record the vision and inscribe it on tablets that the one who reads it may run. For the vision is yet for the appointed time; it hastens toward the goal and it will not fail. Though it tarries, wait for it; for it will certainly come, it will not delay.**
>
> **– Habakkuk 2:2-3**

It anchors the strategic plan in something concrete.

Writing the vision and using language that declares it to be an accomplished fact is not mere semantics. It commits the organization to creating something measurable and substantive. It forces the leadership to be accountable to real and visible outcomes. In addition, it invites actionable behavior, holding up a standard for leaders, employers and other constituents to work toward.

It Publicly Declares the Intent of the Organization.

Organizations do not exist merely for themselves. Whether for-profit, not-for-profit, governmental, or family-owned, there is always an effect on the public. When an organization publishes its vision, it is declaring both its right to engage the public and its responsibility to serve the public. Those who declare their intent publicly tend to be those who recognize that responsibility accompanies rights. By painting a clear vision of the vision – that is, the outcome of their activities, those organizations are engaging in a transparency that allows the public to evaluate their effectiveness in using resources. Do the ends justify the means?

This does have a downside in that no matter how laudable you think the values and vision are, there will be those who will disagree with them and challenge your right to work toward creating such a future. This is why we push so hard to equip organizations to hear the voice of the Holy Spirit who is representing the very will of God. There will still be those who disagree with the envisioned future, but if you have been diligent in examining your personal and corporate purity and your motives, you will at least have the confidence that you have birthed the planning process with the public good at heart. (See Chapter Four).

It Creates an Outlet for People's Desire to Serve a Bigger Goal.

It is well established in leadership literature that leaders cannot motivate followers. What they can do is create an environment in which the followers motivate themselves. When leaders cast a vision that is compelling, exciting and concrete, people want to be a part of it. This is key to both recruitment and retention of good employees.

One of our remodeling clients has a top-notch foreman whose lifelong dream had been to work for the wind generator farms. To him it represented prestige and high salary. Finally, a position came up, but he turned it down. He explained to our client that even though it was what he always wanted, it still felt right to stay with the remodeling company where they were doing something to change people's lives and to improve people's families. The company vision was a strong enough draw to counteract the temptation of high salary in a high profile job.

A well-crafted vision draws people to something bigger than themselves and their needs. Another client of ours is a successful Asian grocery store with about 100 employees. Because 80% of them are Buddhists, our client, who believes the business belongs to God, chose to cast the vision without using any Christian terms. In presenting it, he explained that they aren't about selling food, but about using food to transform the lives of everyone they meet. Several of the Buddhist employees came to him and said that if that's what they were about, they would like to organize groups from the store to go pack meals for Feed My Starving Children. He readily agreed, knowing that in the process of their living out the vision, they would also be hearing a presentation of the gospel each time they went.

Identifying God's Vision

Implementation Suggestions

(This may be a good point to pause and reflect and write down the ideas that are stirring in your head and heart).

1.　Start with His Values

Look again at that list of values you created after the last chapter. Examine them to see common threads running through them. Note also where they are different and how many subject areas they cover.

2.　Ask Questions about the Outcome of His Values

Questions we find useful include:

If all of God's values were in place, what would this sphere He has us working in look like?

How would His "good and perfect will" manifest itself in this area?

How would the experts in our field know when success has been achieved?

If a journalist were to do a piece on the perfect conditions in our sphere, how would they be described?

3.　Record the Vision

Start with a series of phrases that capture the outcome of the values in various subject areas. For example, young adults with strong, marketable skills;

colleges and universities teaching moral decision making; fathers' hearts turned to their children; etc.

When you feel you have captured them all, begin to craft them into sentences describing the future – as if it were already happening. Use present tense verbs. This is an example from the Bishop Gamanywa Foundation in Tanzania:

> "10 million youth have access to 10 million hectares of land with sustainable investments whose proceeds remain in the hands of Tanzanians."

While the values are not listed individually, you can infer from this vision statement that it is important that the resulting prosperity remains in the country. Notice the present tense even though the plan is not expected to be completed for 15 years.

And from the Tanzania Institute of Talents in Dar es Salaam, we see an example of a vision that encompasses several different constituencies:

Our Institute...

• Is well-known and respected in the community.

• Occupies attractive space with the latest technologies and materials.

• Embodies and manifests God's love, power and grace in the world.

• Is an attractive force in challenging wrong thinking in every sector.

Students...

- Are equipped and changing the world around them with competence and confidence.

- Know and walk in their giftedness.

- Are mature and wise in application of their knowledge.

- Are successful financially, morally and relationally.

Teachers...

- Are enjoying and are positively challenged by their work.

- Are well compensated.

- Are change agents for transformation.

The Community...

- People who interact with our institute, its students and teachers are influenced to know and receive the Lord.

Chapter Six

Your Mission Emerges

Remember the three major questions that have to be asked and answered in Upside-Down Strategic Planning?

What are God's values?

If all of those values were in place, what would our sphere of influence look like? That is, what is God's vision?

What part do we play in realizing that vision? That is, what is our mission?

Well, congratulations. You have finished the first two. You know what's on God's heart and you know the future that He sees for the sphere of influence in which He has placed you – His values, His vision. Now the remaining question is your mission. In accomplishing the fullness of the future He has ordained, what task is He giving you?

Mission is a word derived from the Latin word *mittere*, which means to send. Mission is a sending out. The word has come to mean a task we perform or a function we fulfil, and it certainly means that. But focus for a moment on its origin and we see that if it is a sending out, someone other than us must be doing the sending. In this sense, mission takes on a larger meaning. It implies that the sending out fits into some larger purpose.

Whatever area of operation you sought God's vision for – say, for example, reforming home school education – it is still just a small part of His bigger vision for childhood education. Add to that adult education, remedial education, technical education and special education and the vision is even larger. And His vision is for the whole world, while He may have you operating in a limited geographical area. Your mission flows out of what God has destined for His people, which is much greater than anything you and I can wrap our minds around.

With permission, ©Atlasowa, Creative Commons Attribution

But that doesn't mean your mission within that smaller vision of home school education isn't important. Rather, you are sent into that arena because it is important. Your mission fits into a grand plan to make all things right, to restore God's values to the world.

The Christian reader will understand that God's mission has already been accomplished in Christ.

"I glorified You on the earth, having accomplished the work which You have given Me to do. (John 17:4)

... He said, "It is finished!" And He bowed His head and gave up His spirit. (John 19:30)

God's mission was to install the Kingdom of God in the hearts of men, in this world, in this time. When asked about when the Kingdom would come, Jesus answered,

"Nor will they say, 'Look, here it is!' or, 'There it is!' For behold, the kingdom of God is in your midst." (Luke 17:21)

Jesus' mission was to permanently establish the Kingdom in the hearts of men. He left us with the mission of revealing that Kingdom. As His saving love is demonstrated through our relationships in the world, people's eyes will be opened so that they can see the Kingdom among them, which is "righteousness, peace and joy in the Holy Spirit." (Romans 14:17)

"And I confer on you a kingdom, just as my Father conferred one on me," (Luke 22:29-NIV)

"As You sent Me into the world, I also have sent them into the world." (John 17:18)

That sounds to me like a mission to fulfil the values and vision of God.

We have been tasked with restoring all that has been redeemed. Jesus noted in His prayer to the Father that His mission has been entrusted to us until His return.

In Chapter Four we discussed the Luke 19 account of the man who went away to be crowned king and left the administration of his affairs in the hands of his servants. Upon his return some of his servants turned over to him an expansion of the resources with which he had entrusted them. They had understood their "sending" as part of his bigger mission and therefore they stewarded and built his resources. To those servants, the master gave authority to rule over the cities in his kingdom.

Unless our mission fits into God's vision, it is meaningless and counterproductive.

> But He [Jesus] turned and said to Peter, "Get behind Me, Satan! You are a stumbling block to Me; for you are not setting your mind on God's interests, but man's." (Matthew 16:23)

Understanding values and vision from God's viewpoint changes everything. No longer are you working only for your own, limited ends. No longer are you bound by your own thinking, worldview, personality, resources, etc. You have signed on to what Dennis Peacocke refers to as "Almighty and Sons." You have a franchise in the family business owned by God, Himself. *(Doing Business God's Way*, Rebuild, Santa Rosa, CA 1995). The franchisor, God, wants you to succeed in your franchise, because your success advances the visibility, the reach, and the power of the family business.

For many organizations, their mission is directly related to the values and vision that birthed them. For example, the Tanzania Institute for Talents that we introduced in the last chapter adopted a mission that changed very little after they had finished this Upside-Down Strategic Planning.

> "Our Institute is a unique, professional development center, programmed to explore the God-given talents of individuals, freeing their minds of limiting ideas so as to discover their true self. Graduates and Teachers apply practical truth and competence in their chosen line of study so that they transform and prosper their sphere of influence."

Whether you are Christian or not, it is important that you root your mission in the bigger vision; that you see how it is connected to a larger world view. Understanding your mission's importance to something bigger gives it much greater appeal and urgency.

Are you having trouble seeing your mission that way? Depending on the area in which you work, it can be difficult. We have a client who sells heavy duty truck springs and another who has a trucking company. It's hard to see those as world-transforming. Another client develops websites and smartphone apps. How does that fit into a world-changing vision?

In cases like those, you can begin to see your mission as providing a springboard for a second, larger mission. The truck spring distributor and his wife have a passion for improving marriages. They find numerous opportunities in talking to end users, other dealers and suppliers to model their own marriage and open up dialogue about healthy relationships. The trucking company owner has a heart for ex-prisoners and addicts re-entering society. He uses his company as an outlet for them to learn job skills and to make responsible decisions about money. The app developer feels especially called to speak into young men's lives about purity and morality. The field is ripe with young coders and he finds ample opportunity to build relationships.

(It is important to note here, that not all of these mission objectives may be publicly declared. Some are held internally, giving meaning and incentive to the employees. Stating them externally may or may not be the best way to accomplish them).

If you did a good job in the values and vision section, you became aware of a call on your life, something for which you feel you are being sent. How can you use your organization's immediate mission to support that calling? Be intentional about articulating the connections between what you do and what your broader mission in life is.

Everything that follows in your strategic planning is driven by and supports God's Kingdom mission. You will likely find it necessary to realign your product or service offering with this mission. Leadership, marketing and sales, hiring, compensation, supply chain relationships, customer service may all have to be retooled to accomplish what God has in mind for your company or organization. At the very least, you will want confirmation that your current direction and organization are aligned with the Kingdom mission.

Identifying Your Mission

Implementation Suggestions

1.   "Why" Drives the "What"

Go back over Values and Vision. We suggest you make a large chart on which you prominently display your finished copy of both. Include what you have learned about your particular call in life, even if it doesn't seem to be associated with the values and vision.

2.   Ask Questions About How the Vision Could be Realized.

Questions we find useful include:

In what areas do we seem to be drawing very close to fulfilling the "perfect" vision?

Are there activities we could be involved in that would help move the world closer to it?

(For existing organizations) How is our current mission connected to the values and vision?

(For new organizations) What could we be doing to further the values and vision?

In what ways do our current activities help or hinder moving toward that perfect vision?

3.   Construct a Visual Connections Chart

Using pins and colored string, or even just colored markers, connect elements in the values and vision with activities you are (or could) be doing. We like using different colors to correspond to different values. It will give you strong visual cues on how well your mission matches which parts of the values and vision statements.

4.   Finally, Craft your New Mission

Write out "what" sentences that support the "why" elements in the values and vision.

Here is an example based on what the truck spring company might come up with in this part of the planning. They already have a clear mission of becoming both the local and regional source for all truck spring parts. In doing this exercise, they realize they are not having as strong an effect on couples as they feel they are called to do.

WHY: In order for us to positively affect marriages in our sphere of influence, our sales mission must include ways of identifying and communicating with couple-owned businesses, and must identify solid business reasons for improving marriage relationships.

WHAT: Our mission will include a focus on sharing practical advice for improving bottom-line results as well as employee satisfaction for truck repair shops and dealerships.

This addition in mission will lead to the steps you will learn in the following chapters about the alternative to SWOT statements, and goals, strategies and action plans. (SWOT stands for Strengths, Weaknesses, Opportunities, and Threats.)

Take all the "what" statements you have developed and craft them into your complete mission statement.

5. Writing it Down

There are many different ways you can write your mission statement. The personality you and your organization have will help determine what will work best for you. We suggest a couple thoughts to help guide you.

Keep it short. Remember that the purpose of the mission is twofold – to identify actions that accomplish the vision and to rally yourself and your employees to live that vision through your actions.

Be sure you can tie every part of your mission back to relevant values and vision statements.

Customize the words to your audience. If your mission is to be used largely internally, focus the wording on your own employees or volunteers. If it is to be used to communicate with the public, use language that will engage them.

Consider boiling down the finished statement into a few short words that capture the main values or the most important part of your vision. Well known examples include Ford Motor Company's "Quality is Job One" and Staples Office Supplies' "That Was Easy."

Chapter Seven

The Big Step Beyond the Values, Vision and Mission

Of course, a strategic plan is not complete with just its vision and mission. Vision and mission exist to give direction to the action we are to take. The corporate model of strategic planning moves into a SWOT analysis (assessing Strengths, Weaknesses, Opportunities and Threats), followed by the creation of goals, strategies and plans. Upside-Down Strategic Planning, too, contains all of those elements – though the process and application are different than in the corporate model.

Consider this account of how The Promised Land came to the Israelites.

God had established a clear mission for Moses and his people based on God's values – His feelings for the Israelites and His determination to rescue them and favor them as His people in a land flowing with milk and honey. The mission was, "go and take this land" (in Exodus 3:7-10) How Moses responds exposes the shortcomings of man's planning and sets a Spirit-led model for this part of the planning process. In Numbers 13:2, the Lord commands Moses, "Send some men to explore the land of Canaan, which I am giving to the Israelites."

Why was God sending out a reconnaissance team? Surely He knew what and who was in the land. He already told Moses it was a rich land. He described the vision in the present tense as "a land flowing with milk and honey." He had already repeated three times that He was giving the land to the Israelites. So God didn't need a scouting report.

Why did God tell Moses to explore? Could it be that He wanted to show them the gift He was giving them? To have them see His vision the same way He saw it – as a marvelous gift to be enjoyed? Moses, however, embellished on God's instructions. Moses said,

> "Go up through the Negev and on into the hill country. See what the land is like and whether the people who live there are strong or weak, few or many. What kind of land do they live in? Is it good or bad? What kind of towns do they live in? Are they unwalled or fortified? How is the soil? Is it fertile or poor? Are there trees in it or not? Do your best to bring back some of the fruit of the land." (Numbers 13:17-20)

Rather than having faith in God's vision, Moses redefined the vision by his restatement of the mission. He unknowingly instilled doubt about the gift. He saw the Promised Land as an obstacle to overcome. He focused on the threats therein. He placed his own intellect and leadership experience above that of God. He departed from Spirit-led planning by trying to identify what he and his team would have to do, rather than what God had already done.

Moses engaged what traditional strategic planning calls a SWOT analysis. He sent in the spies to see how the Israelites' strengths and weaknesses stacked up against the opportunities and threats they would encounter.

A SWOT analysis starts with the assumption that the vision is only obtainable by strategically offsetting the external threats and our internal weaknesses with the vagaries of environmental opportunities and our own strengths.

Look at the Results of Moses' SWOT Analysis:

When they returned from spying out the land, at the end of forty days, they proceeded to come to Moses and Aaron ...and they brought back word to them and to all the congregation and showed them the fruit of the land. Thus they told him, and said, "We went in to the land where you sent us; and it certainly does flow with milk and honey, and this is its fruit.

"Nevertheless, the people who live in the land are strong, and the cities are fortified and very large; and moreover, we saw the descendants of Anak there. Amalek is living in the land of the Negev and the Hittites and the Jebusites and the Amorites are living in the hill country, and the Canaanites are living by the sea and by the side of the Jordan.

... "We are not able to go up against the people, for they are too strong for us."

So they gave out to the sons of Israel a bad report of the land which they had spied out, saying, "The land through which we have gone, in spying it out, is a land that devours its inhabitants; and all the people whom we saw in it are men of great size.

"There also we saw the Nephilim (the sons of Anak are part of the Nephilim); and we became like grasshoppers in our own sight, and so we were in their sight." (Numbers 13:25-29, 31-33)

One sentence described what God had promised them followed by a recitation of all the barriers to receiving it. As the account goes on, we see that 10 out of 12 spies focused on the threats and their own weaknesses, while only two focused on God's promise and relied on His character. The negative report filled the entire population with fear and they refused to enter into the land and grasp the vision. The result? They wandered in the desert for 40 years until the entire generation of doubting, fearful people died out.

Moses missed an opportunity here. He lost a chance to empower an entire generation into living a future that was marked by excellence. He had two leaders who understood the power of faith in the One who imparts vision, but he allowed himself to be swayed by those who mistook their own limitations for the potential to define the future.

God's model for planning does not include a SWOT analysis. There's nothing really wrong with that approach – it's just not God's best for us. Isaiah 55:8 says, "'For my thoughts are not your thoughts, neither are your ways my ways' declares the Lord."

Some might say this contradicts the "count the cost" process described in Luke 14:28-30 and even eliminates the need for planning. No. *Before* you make a commitment to the Lord is the time to count the cost. Once we have made the commitment, we are to be all in, trusting completely in the Lord. As you will see, the remaining planning steps are for the purpose of taking hold of that which is already ours by virtue of the vision.

"OFF" Statements

There is an alternative to SWOT that fits quite well into the Upside-Down Strategic Planning model. Like any good model it must have an acronym, so we have named it "OFF." It stands for "Opportunities For Faith." Or if you're more comfortable with it, "On Forging the Future," or "Owning Future Facts." The initials aren't important, but the concept is.

OFF means walking into the vision with an absolute confidence that it belongs to us.

OFF analysis looks something like this. Focusing on God's vision for the future, we identify all those things God would want us walking into, those

Every age needs men who will redeem the time by living with a vision of the things that are to be. – Adlai E. Stevenson

situations and people He sees us in the midst of. We accept God's vision for our organization and seek His promises in the Word that allow us to have faith for that vision. We pray into those situations by owning and declaring those promises. In this way, we create a list of opportunities for faith around which we will set goals, strategies and action plans. Another example might be helpful.

When Linda and I caught God's vision for Market 70, we saw that He had us working internationally with multi-million dollar companies and organizations. He had the Market 70 materials being used by companies all over the world.

Uh, excuse me, reality check! We didn't know one person who had more than a $10 million dollar company. We had no international contacts in business. And the Market 70 materials didn't exist! These were all Opportunities For Faith. We began walking into His vision by praying. As we did so, He brought to our minds Scriptures that promised He would deliver nations to us. Our intercessors received word that we would be ministering internationally. People we didn't even know told us that in prayer, they saw us dealing with governments. God's Word assured us He would "establish the work of our hands." We were reminded that He would share His counsel with us and reveal things we could not know. As we believed Him for His provision and for His direct guidance into His vision, we immediately began to see things happen.

Are you beginning to see the value of OFF over SWOT? Focusing on God's opportunities for faith brings us directly into action steps that are undergirded by divine will and promise. It keeps our attention on the outcome – the vision – rather than on the impediments, weaknesses, barriers, etc. Oh, they are still there, to be sure. And we are still aware of them. But they enter our planning process as a "done deal" rather than as something in our path. SWOT analysis is linear, temporal and concrete. OFF is non-linear, dynamic, and eternal (in that it is not time bound) and abstract. SWOT relies on our own efforts while OFF relies on what God is doing.

SWOT places management and employees in a position of working toward an uncertain end because of the focus on overcoming the present obstacles. Though we may do our best to motivate ourselves and direct our strengths, gifts and talents to removing or overcoming those obstacles, our current existence is still defined by them. We are still "here." OFF has the advantage of creating a future reality now, in the present. Management and employees own and embrace and begin living the future reality today, in spite of obstacles.

Does that sound all metaphysical and theoretical? Let us make it real for you.

Which scenario would you prefer? Do you want employees who truly believe and act like they are totally empowered to deliver excellent customer service in spite of the numerous logistical obstacles your company faces in doing so? Or do you want employees who always hesitate, waffle and make excuses with customers because they are still "working out the kinks?" In the former situation, your staff are already living in the vision of excellent, uninhibited customer service. Yes, it leaves management in the position of scrambling behind the scenes to keep up with customer needs, but the customers themselves feel as if they are in competent, caring hands.

Switching from SWOT to OFF is just good leadership. It is the role of the leader to cast a vision that others believe in, aspire to and are encouraged and empowered by. It is the role of the leader to establish followers in an environment in which their strengths and talents will be applied to experiencing success. OFF directs all their knowledge, skill and charisma into walking into the reality of the future they envision.

Moving from SWOT to OFF

Of all the concepts we teach in the Upside-Down Strategic Planning model, this is the most difficult for people to grasp. It is particularly difficult for people with the personality styles characterized by cautious, quality-oriented characteristics and those who are described more by dominance, results and action. But all of us have a sense of wanting to be in control. And that means knowing all the possible glitches that could possible spring up.

The Israelites wanted to know what they were going to do when they came up against the walled cities, the huge soldiers and the hilly countryside that spelled ambush. They wanted to know how they were going to deal with a people they had only heard stories and rumors about.

> **"Fear punches holes in your eyes so that you don't see the future clearly. Faith enlarges your vision to behold your destiny."**
>
> — Israelmore Ayivor, Leaders' Ladder

OFF demands that we walk by faith. "Now faith is the assurance of things hoped for, the conviction of things not seen." (Heb 11:1) Faith relies on someone or something bigger than ourselves – that universal vision or God.

This will test the work you did in listening for the deepest, most important **values**. It will cause you to ponder anew the **vision** created from the perfect application of those values. And it will cause you to question your **mission** and how well you have heard the call on your life and your organization.

When you've done this, you will come to a conviction that the vision as presented to you is a sure thing. Your mission will launch you into walking into that part of the vision that is within your sphere of influence. Your eyes will be set on the outcome, not on the journey. You will not suffer the fear that comes from focusing on the barriers to reaching the goal.

OFF – How Does it Work?

Developing an OFF statement is simply declaring what must be in place in order for the vision to be realized. Some of our clients have described this as a "mini-vision." Don't bite off more than you can chew. We recommend working on only two OFF statements at a time.

Develop goals, strategies and action plans around the OFF statement(s) and begin work on them immediately. As you begin to see the circumstances described in the OFF statement unfold, it is evidence that the realization of the bigger vision is drawing closer. But the vision is, by definition, huge. The full vision is probably at least five-years out and may not be seen even in a lifetime.

The next step, then, is to define another OFF statement. Ask yourself the question again, "What's the next big set of conditions that must exist in order for us to move closer to the vision?" That OFF statement, then, becomes the base for the next set of goals, strategies and action plans. The strategic planning process continues from there.

It's called "successive approximation," that is, getting closer and closer to the ultimate end by moving into it a little bit at a time.

The following illustration is a representation of an actual client's work, though it is neither complete nor literal. I have amended and simplified it to work as an example of creating OFF statements.

We used Upside-Down Strategic Planning with a county mental health agency. Of course, we did not present it from a Christian standpoint, but got excellent participation when we engaged staff and leaders around values. They filled two whiteboards with what they all agreed on were the highest values in creating a strong, integrated mental health system.

They were able to quickly identify the vision – what the county's mental health environment would look like if all those values were in place. They easily created a vision statement made up of about seven sentences that defined the future in the present tense.

Then they re-examined their own mission – a specific part of realizing that vision in that it was to serve as an advisory body to the county board on mental health issues, practices, policy and legislation.

They then went on to develop OFF statements. They asked the question, "What two or three things absolutely have to be in place for our vision to be realized?"

Part of the vision stated, *"General Practitioners and Family Practice clinics routinely screen for and recognize signs of chronic mental illness and there is clear and easy access into the mental health treatment system for those patients."*

The vision is huge. There is a tremendous gap between today's reality and this ideal future.

The OFF statement that flowed out of that was a mini-vision, an intermediate reality that must be in place before the greater vision would be fully realized. *"GPs and Family Practice physicians have comprehensive and easy screening tools that coincide with the treatment system's requirements for access and payment."*

A second OFF statement that flowed out was around the funding. *"The County Board has clear and compelling information to support ample funding for early detection and referral mechanisms between the County and private providers."*

The vision would still not be fully realized by the fulfillment of these two OFF statements, but it would be far closer to being a reality.

A separate planning session was then planned to create the goals, strategies and action plans to support these two OFF statements. The group left the meeting encouraged and focused on creating actions that would accomplish a key part of the vision.

In past planning efforts, they had always used SWOT analysis: identifying gaps in the mental health system and performing a gap analysis to come up with an agenda for their future actions. The discussion around gaps was discouraging because it encompassed so much more that was completely outside the county's sphere of influence, so the results were always disappointing. The resulting goals and strategies were too complex and required far more resources than they could possibly muster.

By identifying OFF statements, they had a clear direction for action planning within an arena over which they had input and influence.

In the following Implementation page we summarize the process of creating OFF statements.

OFF Statements

Implementation Suggestions

1.   God-sized Goals

Be sure all your planning participants understand the idea of OFF statements. They are seeing the future and identifying those God-sized goals that must be accomplished so that the vision is fulfilled. OFF statements look past the barriers to the vision to those things that open up the vision to reality.

2.   Ask Questions to Identify OFF

Questions that we recommend include the following:

What events or situations would have to be in place before the vision could be fully realized?

If you were looking back on the finished vision, what would be reported as that which ushered in the changed reality?

3.   Record the OFF Statements

Choose only one or two Opportunities For Faith to work on. That means you must identify the most important conditions for change. Too many and you will be overwhelmed.

4.   Identify Measures of Change

How do you know if your strategic actions are making a difference? This is often a difficult step because change is sometimes difficult to measure, but everything can be measured if you apply yourselves to the task. Some things can be measured by direct observation while other things can be measured by "proxy." We can look at things that are indications of change taking place. If you're not familiar with proxy measures, or if you are unsure how to get started with identifying them for the OFF statements you have, we suggest you read our treatment of the subject on our website. You will find the article under Internal Transformation and then Reaping Transformation. The URL is:

http://www.market70.com/index.php/step-8-reaping-transformation/reaping-transformation

5.   Write New OFF Statements

When the events or situations you described in the OFF statement has come to pass, go back to the values, vision and mission and identify the next God-sized goal by asking the questions in Suggestion 2 again. Then follow up with a new set of goals, strategies and actions that will allow you to "walk into" that future reality.

Chapter Eight

Values and Vision into Action

Goals, Strategies and Action Plans

"Finally," you are probably saying. "We get to something we're familiar with." Well, yes and no. This portion of Upside-Down Strategic Planning parallels the corporate model closer than all the other pieces so far. The differences are seen in how your work flows out of and supports the big vision with which you started.

The steps, while linear in structure, are faith-based actions that support the realization of the values' outcome. At this point in the process, you heart has become one with God's heart. You have committed yourself totally to His vision and you are actually creating what already exists in the sight of God. Or in words for those who are not seeing this spiritually, you have allowed yourself to be led by the overarching values that gave birth to a vision of the future that you embrace as a factual reality.

You will now begin to see these well-known Scriptures come alive:

"Commit to the LORD whatever you do, and he will establish your plans." (Proverbs 16:3)

"Delight yourself in the LORD and he will give you the desires of your heart. Commit your way to the LORD; trust in him and he will do this: He will make your righteousness shine like the dawn, the justice of your cause like the noonday sun." (Psalms 37:4-6)

In other words, as your heart and God's heart align, then your plans will be aligned to His vision.

There are many different roads to accomplishing God's vision. He gifted you and your management team and your employees specifically so that they would operate as His "body," each doing a vital part. In addition, He has many different "bodies" living out His values and vision throughout the world. Each is in a unique position to reach specific niche markets and so will approach them with different goals, strategies and action plans. Taken together, they are like a cosmic symphony playing the finished work of the Composer.

Prayerfully approached, the goals, strategies and action plans will be very unique to your organization and its specific mix of talents, personalities and passions. They will, however, be anchored in God's values, vision and mission. As you go through this process, you will be guided into all truth by the Holy Spirit. In each step He will remind you of everything Jesus taught you. (John 14:26) Spirit-led, Upside-Down Strategic Planning is the only way for a Kingdom company or organization to become a powerful, transformation force in the marketplace.

Values	*Specific*
Vision	*General*
Mission	*Specific*
Opportunities For Faith	*General*
Goals	*Specific*
Strategies	*General*
Action Plans	*Specific*

As you create goals, strategies and action plans flowing out of your OFF statements, you should be able to see a clear line running all the way back to the Values and Vision work you did in the beginning. Your work is not your work, it is His work being accomplished through your hands. These activities will bring life to your mission and allow you to actually see the vision growing into reality.

Nomenclature

We start by defining the terms we use. There are different ways of looking at goals and strategies, some stating that goals are bigger than strategies and others stating the opposite. In our minds, it really doesn't matter as long as you stay consistent throughout the process.

An Opportunity for Faith is a general declaration of the condition that will exist as a result of your executed plan.

A goal is a specific desired result toward which you direct your activities.

A strategy is a general method for achieving a goal.

An action plan is a set of specific steps in carrying out the strategy.

Notice the alternating description of these terms between general and specific. This mirrors the interaction we encountered with the development of the values, vision and mission. We began by listening for and listing out the detailed list of values that form a broad future vision. Our specific mission flowed out of that. The contrast between general and specific becomes very clear with the goals, strategies and action plans.

Goals

In Chapter Three we talked about the factors in planning that result in plans that sit on the shelf. Setting goals well is the key to creating a plan that overcomes many of those factors.

A goal that is too narrow will fail to engage the stakeholders in anything of substance.

A goal written with insufficient depth of knowledge from a self-reliant staff will be shallow and lack enough of a challenge to engage significant action.

A goal that is too lofty to attain in any realistic timeframe will immediately be seen as grandiose and without hope of accomplishing.

A goal in simple compliance with a rule or with outside regulators will stand out in that there is no clear line back to the values and vision.

So, how do you assure that your plans both follow logically from the values, vision and mission and create a clear direction for the strategies and action plans?

Most planners recommend **S.M.A.R.T.** goals, an idea usually attributed to Peter Drucker in the early 1980's. Well-written goals should meet these criteria:

Specific – targeted and focused on a definable area of desired accomplishment

Measurable – quantifiable or at least containing observable indicators of success

Attainable – realistic and attainable, yet at the same time, requiring a stretch to succeed

Relevant – worthwhile and appropriate to moving the organization to realize the OFF statement

Time-bound – including deadlines and milestones, if appropriate, that contain a sense of urgency

(Some people add two more, Evaluated and Reviewed, which we think are well covered in Measurable and Time-bound).

Our recommendation, in addition to following this time-honored practice of S.M.A.R.T. goals, is that you continue the process of being Spirit-led. Unfortunately, many people finish the OFF statements and then automatically begin relying on their own knowledge and skills. We suggest the continued involvement of your intercessory team, or, for those who are not following this process from a Christian's viewpoint, making sure that those whom you invited to provide the referent knowledge in developing values and vision are still actively involved. (See the Reliance Factor chart in Chapter Two).

The actual process starts with the OFF statements you developed. You have identified a condition that would have to exist in order for the vision to be realized. You must now identify goals to walking into that future reality.

A Real Illustration of Goal Setting

Once again, we believe that providing examples is the best way for people to understand this well enough to put it into practice. In later planning meetings the county agency introduced in the last chapter, may have finished up the process with goals, strategies and action plans similar to what we have written in the next sections.

> **OFF I.** *stated, "GPs and Family Practice physicians have comprehensive and easy screening tools that coincide with the treatment system's requirements for access and payment."*

Goal I.A. *By the opening of the next biennium legislative session, the Mental Health Advisory Council will create a physician-friendly, coordinated mental health screening system meeting Federal, State, and County standards which meets the requirements of health insurance providers.*

OFF II. *stated "The County Board has clear and compelling information to support ample funding for early detection and referral mechanisms between the County and private providers."*

Goal II.A. *By the opening of the next biennium' legislative session, the Mental Health Advisory Council will collect all relevant rules and laws regarding public funding of mental screening and prepare a matrix matching each requirement to the system developed in Goal I.A.*

Goal II.B. *By that same time, the Mental Health Advisory Council will compare the expected cost of the new system with the funding available through the current mechanisms and prepare gap-funding proposals to be presented to the County Board, health insurance providers and private foundations and corporations if necessary.*

Notice the characteristics of S.M.A.R.T. goals are present. The goals are specific and time-bound. The responsibility for achieving them is vested in a specific body for whom such activity is clearly within their mandate. The measurement factors are clearly named in standards, requirements, rules and laws. Further measurement is named in the comparison of expected costs to available funding.

The Advisory Board members can clearly trace the accomplishment of these goals back to the universal values they named and to their vision of a mentally healthy environment. They have already committed themselves to the outcome. The goals now serve as a measurably-specific way to accomplish it.

Strategies

The goals, however carefully crafted, do not provide enough direction to guide the Board's action. This is where strategies come in. Remember, a strategy is a general method for achieving a goal. It answers the question, "How are we going to pull this off?"

Where a goal provides a specific outcome by a specific group of people in a specific time, it still doesn't suggest the "how."

This is where a strategy is so helpful.

Identify one or more strategies that provide a vehicle for reaching each goal. This will be a general approach to carrying out the details in the goal. For example, if your goal were to lose 35 pounds by your birthday next year, you may have two strategies: get more exercise and control your diet. Business strategies work the same way – they provide the general course of action for accomplishing the goal(s).

Action Plans

Strategies are not specific enough by themselves to assure you will meet your goal. This is where action plans come in. Now is the time to flesh out the details. Action plans provide the specifics of who does what, when, and with what resources. Action plans name people, dates, finances, measurable outcomes, frequency of efforts, etc.

Consider the goal of losing 35 pounds by your birthday. You have identified two strategies. The first is to get more exercise. This might include several plans. For example:

- Put aside $25 from each monthly paycheck to join the local gym.
- Exercise 45 minutes per day at least four days per week.
- Enlist your brother to exercise with you to help hold you accountable.
- Every day at work, park in the furthest parking lot and always take the stairs instead of the elevator.

The second strategy is to control your diet. This too, may lead to several action plans:

- Enroll in a cooking healthy course to learn economic and effective ways to reduce fats in your diet.
- Bring lunches to work to eliminate the temptation to eat fast foods.
- Put aside the $4.00/day savings from eating out to reward yourself with buying a new outfit every month.
- Switch to black coffee to avoid excess sugars and fats from creamers.

Action plans are, by their very definition, actionable. Just like goals, they are S.M.A.R.T. They are actions that you can touch, count, observe and measure. They work best if you build in some reward and some method of accountability.

A Real Illustration of Goal Setting (Continued)

To help cement this into place, let us extend the work we started with the county mental health agency by adding strategies and action plans to the goals we have devised for them. We have reprinted the OFF statements and goals so you can see the entire progression.

> **OFF I.** *"GPs and Family Practice physicians have comprehensive and easy screening tools that coincide with the treatment system's requirements for access and payment."*
>
> **Goal I.A.** *By the opening of the next biennium' legislative session, the Mental Health Advisory Council will create a physician-friendly, coordinated mental health screening system meeting Federal, State, and County standards which meets the requirements of health insurance providers.*
>
> **Strategy I.A.1.** *Convene a multi-agency task force to devise the screening.*
>
> **Plan I.A.1.a.** *The Council Chair will announce the forming of the task force at the monthly Directors' meeting and enlist at least five separate agencies willing to meet twice a month to complete the task.*
>
> **Plan I.A.1.b.** *The County Board will provide meeting space, a facilitator and clerical support for the task force.*
>
> **OFF II.** *"The County Board has clear and compelling information to support ample funding for early detection and referral mechanisms between the County and private providers."*

Goal II.A. *By the opening of the next biennium' legislative session, the Mental Health Advisory Council will collect all relevant rules and laws regarding public funding of mental screening and prepare a matrix matching each requirement to the system developed in Goal I.A.*

Strategy II.A.1. *Create an on-line presence to collect, analyze and document information.*

Plan II.A.1.a. *The locally based insurance provider will lend a programmer to create a Task Force website that will be in operation within 30 days.*

Plan II.A.1.b. *The Task Force will market the website in all scheduled mental health trainings and events, both public and private, over the next 60 days.*

Goal II.B. *By that same time, the Mental Health Advisory Council will compare the expected cost of the new system with the funding available through the current mechanisms and prepare gap-funding proposals to be presented to the County Board, health insurance providers and private foundations and corporations if necessary.*

Strategy II.B.1. *Create a sub-committee of financial analysts from both public and private agencies.*

Plan II.B.1.a. *Identify at least five competent analysts and secure agency support for funding their time and presence for monthly meetings over the next six months.*

> ***Plan II.B.1.a.*** *Funnel all the findings of the Task Force in Goal II.A to the sub-committee and perform comparative analyses against current funding schemes. Identify and quantify any gaps and report directly to the County Board.*

From that lengthy example, please notice a few important points. First, the detailed plans are derived from and point back to the values and vision that gave rise the to the Advisory Council's mission. This is vital. If staff and other stakeholders can see the direct connection to the end product, they will be far more motivated to work the plans.

Second, notice the clear difference between the specificity of goals and action plans compared to OFF statements and strategies. If you can keep that clear, the process flows easily and you can maintain that direct line just described. Using some sort of a numbering system helps hold it all together. It could just as well be colors or animals or shapes. The idea is to keep the flow of the plan throughout.

Values

Vision

Mission

Goals   Goals

Strategies   Strategies

Action Plans   Action Plans

Goals, Strategies and Action Plans

Implementation Suggestions

1.   Work with a Smaller Group

These steps take a lot of focused, detailed work which is cumbersome for a large group. If you have been working as an entire staff, it might be best to break down into smaller groups, assigning each a goal or even smaller, a strategy to break down into action plans.

2.   Maintain the Line

Physically and verbally draw the lines. As mentioned in the Implementation Suggestions of Chapter Six, use colored pins and yarn, or colored markers or have each set of values and their subsequent OFF, Goals, Strategies, and Plans recorded on different color paper.

3.   Check the Measures

For each goal and plan, ask the question, "How will we know this was successful?" Strive for concrete measures when you can. If you can't, try to identify proxy measures – that is, conditions that would be present if it were successful. For example, while you may not be able to measure increased income in a high poverty area, you might conclude that a decrease in child malnutrition is an acceptable proxy measure. For a more in-depth understanding of proxy measures in transformation, go to www.market70.com, and look up "Reaping Transformation" under the menu item Internal Transformation.

4.   Put it in Reverse

Finally, when you feel that a particular line of goal accomplishment has been completely planned out, work it backwards to see if the actions, if they were taken, actually accomplish the goal and fulfill the conditions described in the OFF statement.

Chapter Nine

Beyond the Strategic Plan

Strategic planning isn't the only kind of planning. Strategic implies long term planning crucial to fulfilling the vision. There is also annual planning, tactical planning and decision making. Decision  making is really a planning function, too. We will explain the difference between these three and how to use each of them. All of these improve with the Upside-Down method. This chapter presents the Upside-Down model as a practical, "use-on-the-fly" tool that will bring a new level of effectiveness to all your planning.

Annual Planning

The strategic plan is long-range. It defines the attainment of a huge vision, based on highly prized values. Its OFF statements identify situations the organization needs to walk into in order for the vision to be realized.

The goals, strategies and action plans, though, are much less long-range. They represent the time-bound actions the organization will take during a certain period. Throughout the year, the organization will accomplish many of those and will need to define the next level of short-term planning to accomplish those OFF statements.

Yet, annual planning has more importance than just that. In Chapter Two we examined some of the reasons Strategic Planning often fails. We noted several important methods to avoid that failure.

1.   Planning must be a living, dynamic process that evolves through the interaction of the participants, the events and the nature of the mission

2.   We must recognize that our organization is only a part of something much bigger – something we cannot fully grasp, and that we need to constantly be aware of the larger agenda.

3.   To protect ourselves from a sense of hopelessness, the participants must be constantly built up and equipped for success.

4.   Reviewing our efforts with respect to the effects guards against the plan becoming an end in itself. Constantly reminding ourselves of number 2 above, rekindles motivation to "work the plan" so that "the plan works."

5.   Careful attention must be given to whether the plan has become too big for the planners. We must be assured that the plan is still realistic and realizable.

6.   Finally, to keep a Strategic Plan from becoming a bookend, we must see that it still "has legs," that is, that the plan itself plans for continued and productive action.

This section will guide you through the purposes and the ingredients for effective annual planning.

Review the Values, Vision and Mission

In the same way that your organization set aside specific time to identify God's deepest agenda, those overarching values that bring meaning and purpose to the sphere of influence in which you work, repeat the process. It will not take the same amount of time or effort because you won't be starting from nothing, but take the time to really examine and see if you have missed anything, or if the circumstances have highlighted some values as more important than you had originally thought.

Don't skip this step. A manufacturing company we work with had originally heard that a driving value was maintaining a relationship with a key supplier. In reviewing God's heart, they discovered that while that was still important, it was becoming more important to serve a segment of the market that was being underserved because of its inability to pay the high prices for those proprietary materials. They were led to develop their own materials that could be used in that market segment without in any way infringing on the key supplier's presence in the original markets. This has resulted in greatly increased sales and entry into a number of markets they had not been able to serve before.

While God's vision doesn't change, your view and understanding of it might. For a season, you may be focused on a certain part of the vision that defines your mission, however as your organization grows and matures, it might be equipped to focus on a different part or a larger part of the vision for your sphere of influence. For example, look at the changes happening in the food industry as evidence by what your local grocer is selling. (Cage-free eggs, free-range chickens, non-GMO crops, etc.) It appears that the vision for providing food has grown to incorporate a broader vision for environmental protection, sustainability, animal protection, and a reclamation of our natural resources.

If you are a food wholesaler or distributor, you may find your mission shifting as a result of a new understanding of the values and vision affecting your world.

Record and Celebrate Accomplishments

We include this not merely because we value recognition and celebration – although we do think they are highly important to maintaining commitment and motivation. We also believe it has the very practical outcome of ensuring continued success of the plan itself. We often do a great job of identifying what has gone wrong, but we believe that a focus on what we have done right has far more effect on future behavior. Have a party. Publish your results in a newsletter. Publicly congratulate the participants. Share your accomplishments with your customers, suppliers, and supporters.

Recording and celebrating outcomes has the added benefit of sharpening everyone's focus on the values and vision. The annual planning process is the perfect time to orient newcomers to the organization to the bigger agenda in which you are involved.

Finally, this is a good illustration of how the annual planning process introduces new goals, strategies and action plans. If you have heard the values and vision correctly and see them as a driving force, does that not feed into your marketing direction?

Measure Progress on OFF Statements

While OFF statements are usually bigger than what can be accomplished in a year, it's important to measure and record the differences in the last year. If, indeed you have seen the accomplishment of an OFF statement during the year, repeat the process you used to develop OFF statements and hold up the next God-sized goal.

Remember to identify specific metrics with which you can measure success. Go back and review the work you did on measuring success in Chapter Seven.

Reevaluate Hiring and Equipping Policies

As you review the completion of certain goals, strategies and action plans, consider whether you still have the correct mix of personnel, training, tools and policies to accomplish them.

Develop New Goals, Strategies and Action Plans

Finally, to complete your annual planning, you will update the goals and the actions needed to accomplish them.

Tactical Planning

Tactical planning is really nothing more than the planning that takes place as you apply the strategic plan goals, strategies and action plans. It would be almost impossible to sit in a strategic planning session and anticipate every issue that will arise over the next 3-5 years. Tactical planning is the process of addressing ongoing circumstances and assuring that the strategic strategies and action plans are still appropriate to accomplishing the goals.

For example, consider a fictitious airline's strategic plan which has identified as a driving value a commitment to enabling affordable family vacations. They might have a goal of matching competitor price increases only when and if maintaining current prices will result in more than a 5% decrease in year-over-year profits. Suddenly, a major disruption in the labor market in their hub city threatens to push operation costs beyond that threshold. They watch in dismay as their competitors all raise prices to make up for the cost of obtaining available, competent labor. As if the rise in labor costs weren't enough, they are now in danger of losing their own employees to competing airlines willing to pay higher wages.

This is a case for tactical planning. The airline must address the changing circumstances or risk catastrophic losses. What to do?

Review the Values and Vision

A good rule of thumb is to start upside-down. Resist the temptation to *react*, but instead, take the time to go back to your guiding values and vision. What is the overarching, guiding principles that you have discerned in this space? In the case of the fictitious airline, consider not only the value regarding affordability for family, but all the rest as well. What is God (or your inner-most values) driving you toward? What else is important in this sphere of influence and how does it relate? Be willing to look at yet a bigger picture, but don't be quick to abandon what you have seen as the future of your industry or profession.

Questions you and your team might ask yourselves include:

Is there a larger, more important element of the vision that we have overlooked?

Are the circumstances actually pointing us toward confirmation of our original read of the values and vision?

Have we adopted an OFF statement too soon? That is, is there some other major, God-sized goal that must be in place before we will see the vision begin to come into reality?

How do the values point us toward a tactical solution in these adverse circumstances?

What tactics should we adopt in order to protect the values and vision that we have rightly discerned?

Questions like these will lead you back into a goal, strategy and action plan cycle in which you are guided once again by values, vision and your resulting mission rather than being sucked into a reactive stance to circumstances.

Again, consider the airline example. Consider that the team went back to its bedrock values and were once again convinced that the vision of a family-friendly airline industry was still what they were being led to. They reviewed the OFF statement and felt it was indeed the intermediate future that must be in place for the complete fulfillment of the vision. They confirm their mission to be the catalyst that changes the direction of the industry. They review their goals and discover that in order for them to be attained, an additional goal must be added.

They realize that the industry has been moving solidly toward catering to corporate travelers, and that the pleasure-flying public is being disenfranchised. However, their own company has done nothing to galvanize public support against that trend. So they develop tactics that will put their mission squarely into the public eye. Perhaps they devise a multi-faceted tactic:

- appeal to their current employees with a renewed vision,
- the labor unions with incentives for their member families if they would share the burden,
- the public with a strong marketing message aimed at equally sharing the skies with the corporate fliers,
- the FAA with a renewed push for regulations limiting the inequities between business and pleasure flyers
- the oil industry with appeals for fuel price breaks aimed at pleasure-trip airline routes

Effective tactical planning is not reactive, but rather flows from the Upside-Down model, driven by values and vision. To plan any other way is a direct threat to the effectiveness and power of strategic planning. Tactical planning that is not rooted in the original upside-down strategy will result in several if not all of the reasons strategic plans fail that we discussed in Chapter 2.

Decision Making

Every day, on-the-fly, situation-specific decisions. We face them constantly throughout our day. This ongoing process of daily planning – be that corporate or personal – is better served with the  Upside-Down model. We (the authors) have been using the model for more and more "mundane" decisions with increasing success.

The process is basically the same as the model as we have described it, but it happens in a much shorter time frame – sometimes as little as seconds. The frequency with which we apply it results in better results. Practice makes perfect is clearly borne out in this case.

A Real Illustration of Decision Making

Up until recently, we were a two-car family. Our automobiles were both high-mileage cars, long-since paid for. Then one of the cars developed a potentially serious suspension problem. Do we fix it, live with it, or sell it? If we sell it, do we buy another car, and if so, new or used? This is the kind of decision people are faced with often. Maybe it's not as big an issue as a car. Maybe it's a bigger issue involving a major life change or a family member's health. Here's how we handled it.

We scheduled a few minutes together and began by praying. For those of you who aren't into that, begin by getting your mind into a place in which you are open to what comes out of an honest application of the model.

Then we asked ourselves the question that launches the value examination: What is important to God around transportation and our mission? We quickly began to discern those driving values:

- He wants us free to meet mission needs.
- He wants to prosper us and give us the desires of our hearts.
- He wants us to be safe.
- He doesn't want us distracted (by repairs, money worries, etc.)
- He values our giving of time, talent and money
- He want us to live by faith.
- He wants us to live a life worthy of our identity as Kingdom heirs.

There was more, but you get the idea. From the list of values we derived what we saw as God's vision:

We are fully equipped for every good work He calls us to do. Our lifestyle testifies to having our every need met by Him. We are available to travel anywhere in the world and are not tied down by anything. We are actively carrying out our mission without distraction.

From that vision – that present tense, already finished view of our sphere of influence - we perceived that our mission (with regard to transportation) was to rely on Him for whatever transportation we needed.

That led into the God-sized step (OFF statement) of selling the second car without repairing it or buying a replacement.

The whole process took us about 20 minutes. Granted, we've been at this a while and have a lot of practice. But we have used that same process with numerous decisions, some as big as where to live and some as small as whether to take a hotel room to celebrate our anniversary.

Summary

The Upside-Down model is effective in any type of planning. The more you work with it the better you get at using it, and the better results you get from it.

Appendix One

The Tools of Upside-Down Planning

Here are samples of the forms that we use to help guide the process along. Use them as ideas to fashion your own, personalizing them to your own organization. Or, if you prefer, you can download a PDF version of the complete set of the Implementation Suggestions and the corresponding forms from our website, www.market70.com.

Upside-Down Strategic Planning

Values Worksheet

Organization Strategic Plan

Date: _____

Identifying Values

(Be specific. Write down values in behavioral terms, i.e. how the value actually plays out in action.)

What are the core values undergirding everything you are involved in? What is God's heart for your sphere of influence?

What does the Bible say about it?

How does the character of God speak to it?

How has He related to you in the past, bringing you to this point?

Listing Values Group like values together, but be careful not to lose their specificity by categorizing them under broad terms.

Vision Worksheet

Identifying Vision

(Consider a future time, a horizon that has no limitations – at least 5-10 years from now. Write the vision in the present tense, as if it were already in place.)

If all those values were in place; if all were being enacted in reality, what would your sphere of influence look like? Describe the characteristics of your sphere of influence if they were such that your work would no longer be needed.

Write a few brief headlines and a lead paragraph describing the future reality you have just described, above.

Our Ideal Vision of the Future

Mission Worksheet

Identifying Mission

If you have done the previous two steps correctly, you will see that the vision is far bigger than anything you can accomplish. Your mission is a call to specialize; to apply your talents, knowledge and experience to bringing about a part of that big vision.

Having seen the future defined by the core beliefs you have recorded about what is important in your area, what part is your organization to take in bringing it into reality?

Succinctly answer the questions, "Who are we? What do we do? Toward what end? Who benefits?"

Write your mission using action words that clearly move your sphere of influence into some part of the value-defined future you have envisioned.

Our Mission

Finally, you may want to distill your vision into an easy-to-remember, meaningful phrase or sentence that is compelling and exciting.

OFF Worksheet

Identifying Opportunities For Faith

Discuss the rationale behind OFF. If you have a group that will hear better without the faith language, try using "On Forging the Future," or "Opening the Future as Fact."

For the vision you have defined to become a reality, what one or two events or situations would have to be in place before the vision could be fully realized?

If you were looking back on the finished vision, what would be reported as that which ushered in the changed reality?

Write one or two OFF Statements using present tense (as you did in the Vision).

OFF I

OFF II

Goals, Strategies & Plans Worksheet

Identifying Goals, Strategies & Plans

Complete for each OFF statement. Remember that a Goal is specific (SMART as in Chapter 8), a Strategy is a general vehicle for accomplishing the goal, and an Action Plan includes very specific steps for carrying out the Strategy.

OFF I

Goal I.A

Strategy I.A.1

Action Plan I.A.1.a

Person Responsible

Resource/budget amount

Timeline/Milestones

Goal I.B (Add Goals as needed, with appropriate Strategies and Action Plans)

OFF II (Repeat the above process for each OFF Statement)

Appendix Two

A Challenge to a Different World View

Throughout this book we have suggested several ways in which those readers who do not share the Christian world-view might still grasp and value the concepts and ideas of Upside-Down Strategic Planning. Those suggestions came in bits and pieces without an overall theme to help tie them together.

If you count yourself among those who found it hard to see God's values and vision, if the idea of the Holy Spirit was strange or even offensive to you, if seeing an ideal future as a "done deal" sounds like an unrealistic understanding of life, then we invite you to think about the thoughts in these few short pages.

We asked you throughout these chapters to think "bigger picture" if you couldn't think "Christian." We suggested you try to get in touch with what you felt were the most fundamental, important values that guide your work if you couldn't accept Biblical values.

We suggested you identify what would be the perfect future if you couldn't identify with God's vision.

So what is that bigger picture? What are the most basic values? What is the perfect future?

James Choung of InterVarsity has done some great work in connecting with people's inner-most beliefs. He presents us with a challenge around how we see the world and our place in it. He suggests we look at our world today and ask ourselves if it's okay. He says, "None of us thinks that suffering, violence, and oppression are a good thing. We all ache for a better world."

And then he presents a perfectly logical argument. "Just like hunger points to the existence of food, and thirst highlights the reality of water, our ache for a better world seems to point to the possibility that either a better world did exist or that it will one day."

Christians believe that there once was a perfect world, created by an all-knowing and loving God. He had it in mind that we would be supported by and would support that world. We would work together and live together in peace, sustained financially by all that is in that world.

But something went dreadfully wrong. Instead of choosing to live in harmony with each other and with that creation, we began to use each other and the world for our own good at the expense of others and the environment. Our own selfish desires got in the way and we spent thousands of years abusing and corrupting what was designed as a perfect system.

Is it possible to restore the world as designed? The only way to reverse the downward spiral we are in is for someone to remove the corruption we have brought on ourselves and take it out of our hearts and minds and out of the physical creation. We have become hardened to the evil and have become so much a part of it that we can't clean it up. Try as we might, and we do try, nothing we do through government, education, technology, religion or social reform ever works. Our own self-serving nature keeps getting in the way.

This is where Christ comes in. Only someone who has not been infected by the world's corruption can carry it away.

Only someone whose values are perfect and true can be trusted to cast a vision for a perfect and true world.

Only someone who is without any selfish motives can be trusted with leadership in such a hopeless situation.

Only someone whose heart is perfectly pure has the power and influence to repair broken relationships.

Only someone who is all-knowing can share the knowledge we need to see ourselves and our situation clearly.

No world leader in all of history has come even close to being that someone. Except Jesus.

Christians believe that Jesus gave up his divine nature so that he could join us in this broken world. He now invites us to join him in that biggest of all missions – the complete restoration of the world and all who are in it.

We are all invited to be a part of that mission. There are only three things we need to do.

Admit that we are and have been part of the problem.

Trust in the leadership of Christ as the only perfect solution.

Commit ourselves to the mission that he gives us in whatever sphere of influence we find ourselves.

Once we do that, His Spirit (purposely capitalized) provides the power. God's chosen teacher, deputy, power broker, and counselor is the Holy Spirit. After Jesus died, He left his Spirit here to direct the mission until he returns.

So, where are you?

Are you satisfied with the world the way it is?

Can you admit that your own part in creating or at least continuing the problem limits your ability to solve it?

Do you want the power, wisdom and discernment that comes from aligning yourself with the Creator of the universe?

Then just say so. Join a group of other believers who have figured out what you just did – that we can't do it on our own and that we need Jesus and his Spirit to help us.

And now, continue your Upside-Down Strategic Planning knowing that you have placed yourself in the most powerful, influential position possible for the realization of His Vision, your mission.

And if you still don't believe or buy into this, you're your mind and your heart open. Maybe the "bigger picture" you see will become more clear to you.

www.ingramcontent.com/pod-product-compliance
Lightning Source LLC
Chambersburg PA
CBHW070251190526
45169CB00001B/373